The Mandaeans:

Gnostic Astrology as an
Artifact of Cultural Transmission

Maire M. Masco

Tacoma, WA., USA
2012

Published March 21, 2012 by
FLUKE PRESS
6918 East "I" Street, Tacoma, WA 98404
www.flukepress.com

Library of Congress Cataloging-in-Publication Data

Masco, Maire M., 1962-

The Mandaeans: Gnostic Astrology as an Artifact of Cultural
Transmission/Maire M. Masco

Includes bibliographical references.

ISBN–13: 978–1938476006
ISBN–10: 193847600X

1. Mandaeans—Astrology—Gnosticism. 2. History of Science—
Cultural Transmission. 3. Genethlialogical Astrology—Mundane
Astrology

Permission to cite extended sections of the *The Book of the Zodiac
(Sfar Malwaśia)* translated by E.S. Drower, kindly granted by the
Royal Asiatic Society, London, 2012.

Printed in the United States of America.

To Henry Masco, the first of his generation.

And Life is victorious...

.

ACKNOWLEDGEMENTS

I thank the Mandaeans for being so interesting.

I am grateful to the students, faculty, administration, members of the board, and volunteers who can proudly say they were part of the Kepler College of Astrological Arts and Sciences. I offer immense gratitude to the donors whose contributions, large and small, made the academic program at Kepler College possible. *Galaxy class* thanks to Chris Uihlein and the estate of Haloli Richter for endowing subscriptions to the JSTOR and EEBO scholarly research databases. I also thank the AFA, AFAN, ISAR, NCGR and WSAA for their generous scholarships.

I cannot name everyone who contributed to this project, but a few incredible individuals stand out. I thank...

Lynn Bootes, Nicholas Campion, Ronnie Gale Dryer, Demetra George, Dorian Gieseler Greenbaum, Gary Gomes, Charles Häberl, Karen Hamaker–Zondag, Rob Hand, Dennis Harness, James Holden, Judith Holloway, Wendy Katz, Lee Lehman, Hiroshi Masuda, Maria Mateus, Kenneth D. Miller, Margaret Nalbandian, Enid Newberg, Scott Silverman, Stephanie Soibelman, Carol Tebbs, Mark Urban–Lurain, Joanne Wickenburg, and Jolee Worones.

I thank my family: Mary Anne Parmeter, Joe Masco and Shawn Smith, Tom Masco and Vanessa Valdez and Henry Masco, and Cynthia Carlson.

I thank my life partner, Art Chantry. Sorry I was gone for so long.

TABLE OF CONTENTS

ABBREVIATIONS

BOI   *The Book of Instruction in the Elements of the Art of Astrology*, al–Bīrūnī

BTB   *From Astral Omens to Astrology: From Babylon to Bīkāner*, David Pingree

FAN   *The Fihrist of al–Nadim*

GSS   *The Great Stem of Souls*, Jorunn Jacobsen Buckley

MAT   *The Mandaeans: Ancient Texts and Modern People*, Jorunn Jacobsen Buckley

MII   *The Mandaeans of Iraq and Iran*, E. S. Drower

MIT   *Mandaic Incantation Texts*, Edwin M. Yamauchi

OTP   *The Old Testament Pseudepigrapha 2 Volumes*, James H. Charlesworth, ed.

SM   *Sfar Malwasia* (The Book of the Zodiac) E. S. Drower

TLG   *The Mandaeans: The Last Gnostics*, Edmondo Lupieri

YJS   *The Yavanajataka of Sphujidhvaja*

ABSTRACT

The Mandaean gnostic sect of the Persian Gulf dates to the first or second century CE and has survived into contemporary times. Their religious and cultural practices include the use of astrology. The particular form of Mandaean astrology is documented in a manuscript titled "The Book of the Zodiac" or in Mandaic, *Sfar Malwašia*.[1] A facsimile of the original Mandaic manuscript and an English translation were published by E.S. Drower in 1949.[2] Mandaic is a language of the eastern branch of Middle Aramaic, which also includes Syriac and Jewish Babylonian Aramaic.[3] Occasionally the language is classified as Oriental Aramaic because of the inclusion of

---

[1] E. S. Drower, *The Book of the Zodiac (Sfar Malwašia)* D.C. 31, Oriental Translation Fund XXXVI (London: The Royal Asiatic Society, 1949).

[2] Ibid.

[3] M. Sokoloff, *A Dictionary of Jewish Babylonian Aramaic* (Baltimore: Johns Hopkins University Press, 2002), Introduction, 11.

Persian and Arabic loanwords.[4] The *Sfar Malwašia* is a collection of astrology and omen texts that have been compiled to make a functional manual of predictions and pharmacopoeia.[5] The book is used by the Mandaean priesthood for the exclusive benefit of the Mandaean community.[6] The study of the Mandaeans is currently enjoying a minor scholarly revival with the release of several new studies and the re–issue of older titles on the subject.[7] However, the *Sfar Malwašia,* with its esoteric subject matter, has not received much attention.[8] Only two scholarly papers have been published that directly address the *Sfar Malwašia.*[9] The book is a valuable source of

---

[4] Edmondo Lupieri, *The Mandaeans: The Last Gnostics*, trans. Charles Hindley, American Edition (Italian ed. 1993)., Italian Texts and Studies on Religion and Society (Cambridge, U.K.: William B. Eerdmans Publishing Company, 2002), 53.

[5] Ibid., 41.

[6] Drower, *SM*, 1.

[7] Charles G. Häberl, "Review of Das Mandäische Fest Der Schalttage by Bogdan BurteaReview," *Journal of the American Oriental Society* 127, no. 2 (April 1, 2007): 208.

[8] Jorunn Jacobsen Buckley, *The Mandaeans: Ancient Texts and Modern People* (Oxford University Press, 2002), 15, n. 58; Jorunn Jacobsen Buckley, *The Great Stem of Souls: Reconstructing Mandaean History* (Piscataway, NJ: Gorgias Press, 2005), opinion repeated, 120, n. 34.

[9] Francesca Rochberg, *In the Path of the Moon: Babylonian Celestial Divination and Its Legacy* (Leiden: Brill, 2010), Ch. 11 "The Babylonian Origins of the Mandaean Book of the Zodiac." (Originally published in *ARAM* 11–12 (1999–2000), 237–247. Traces the Babylonian sources; JoAnn Scurlock, "Sorcery in the Stars: STT 300, BRM 4.19-20 and the Mandaic Book of the Zodiac," *Archiv Für Orientforschung* 51 (2006 2005): Compares magical rites found on cuneiform tablets. My gratitude to D.G. Greenbaum for sharing this article with me.

information about the historical development of astrology, and a useful document in the study of cultural transmission. The purpose of this thesis is to clarify, where possible, the astrological practices found in the *Sfar Malwaśia*. Material that has been dismissed as corrupt or unintelligible is given value by the appropriate astrological context and explanation, and new questions are raised that are apparent only when treating the work as a piece of astrological literature rather than simply part of the Mandaean religious canon. The influence of Gnosticism on the astrological practices of the Mandaeans is considered. The importance of Mandaean astrology in the history of astrology is established, with examples of genethlialogical and political astrological techniques.[10]

The syncretic and transitional nature of Mandaean astrology is particularly useful to illustrate the transmission of intellectual concepts between occidental and oriental cultures occurring in the Persian Gulf region in the classical and medieval periods. The evidence of mundane astrological houses indicates a time after the development of Babylonian astral divination, yet the Babylonian omen material is fully present and sometimes copied exactly from cuneiform texts.[11] The twelve–fold house system of Hellenistic astrology is used throughout the material, but the Egyptian system of decans is also found in multiple sections. The astrological physiognomy recorded by the Mandaeans is similar, and may even be contemporary with material found in the Nag Hammadi and Dead Sea Scroll literature. The practice of separate horoscopes for men and women is found in *Jyotisha*, or Indian astrology. The annual predictions for the year are similar to practices found in Egypt and Palestine, as well as Persian calculations found in Tajik astrology. Techniques specifically

---

[10] The iatromathematical (medical) astrology and omen interpretations found in the *Sfar Malwaśia* are not addressed in this paper.

[11] Rochberg, *In the Path of the Moon*, 231 (compare Iqqur īpus 77:1–6 and *SM* 210).

described as Greek in the text are found, in addition to Sassanian and Persian cyclical theories.[12]

The Mandaean people existed as a marginal or persecuted sub–group in their homeland from the second century CE until the 1990s.[13] Their literature, safely protected by scribal copyists over the centuries, is useful in many areas of scholarly study, including religious and cultural studies.[14] As the scholar Cyrus Gordon (American, 1908–2001) proclaimed, "Mandaic should be studied in depth by several circles of scholars, of whom the Gnostics are only one."[15] The primary focus of this study is the astrological material and what it can teach us about the development of astrology in the classical and medieval periods. The archeologist Franz Cumont (Belgium, 1868–1947) called astrology a "sidereal mysticism," which he speculated was originally practiced by an intellectual *élite*.[16] In the *Sfar Malwašia* we find an elite practice, gleaned from many traditions, adapted for the common people. This thesis will demonstrate how and why the Mandaean *Sfar Malwašia* can be treated as historical evidence, albeit in the form of astrology, of cultural transmission.

---

[12] This is not a reference to the Greek language, but to the astrological techniques ascribed to Greek norms compared to indigenous Mesopotamian techniques.

[13] Christa Müller-Kessler, "The Mandaeans and the Question of Their Origin," *Aram* 16 (2004): 1, 53.

[14] Jonas C. Greenfield, "A Mandaic Miscellany," *Journal of the American Oriental Society* 104, no. 1 (January 1, 1984): 81–85; Edwin M. Yamauchi, "The Present Status of Mandaean Studies," *Journal of Near Eastern Studies* 25, no. 2 (April 1, 1966): 88–96. These articles provide examples of cross–disciplinary applications of Mandaean literature.

[15] Cyrus H. Gordon, "Review: Mandaeism by Kurt Rudolph," *Journal of the American Oriental Society* 99, no. 3 (July 1, 1979): 476.

[16] Franz Cumont, *Astrology and Religion Among the Greeks and Romans*, (1912) ed. (New York: Dover, 1960), 77.

ABSTRACT

The Mandaeans lived in the marshlands created by the confluence of the Tigris and Euphrates rivers. This area falls in the eastern portion of the Fertile Crescent, a concept introduced by the orientalist James Henry Breasted (American, 1865–1935).[17] The area is currently under Iraqi control, but the indigenous Mandaean population extends into modern Iran. Sumer and Akkad describe historical periods and kingdoms, while Babylonia and Southern Mesopotamia describe the geographic territory between the Tigris and Euphrates rivers.[18] The land occupied by the Mandaean people can be described as the Persian Gulf region.

Transliterated Mandaic words are given in **bold**. Akkadian, Sumerian, Greek, Pahlavi, Sanskrit, and Arabic terms are given in *italic*. Definitions and alternate spellings are provided when relevant. A perennial challenge when working with cross–cultural terminology is the varying treatment found in different transliterations. Consistent usage is endeavored but not always achieved. Astrological terms are particularly difficult. Most secondary sources use transliterated terms that become accepted into the nomenclature, and where the term inevitably becomes corrupt over time, e.g., *hōroskopos* becomes *horoscope*. Every attempt is made to be consistent with the use of diacritical markings; however, direct quotations will show variation.

---

[17] Albert T. Clay, "The So-Called Fertile Crescent and Desert Bay," *Journal of the American Oriental Society* 44 (January 1, 1924): 186.

[18] Juris Zarins, "The Early Settlement of Southern Mesopotamia: A Review of Recent Historical, Geological, and Archaeological Research," *Journal of the American Oriental Society* 112, no. 1 (January 1, 1992): 55.

1 INTRODUCTION TO MANDAEAN STUDIES

1.1. SCHOLARLY TREATMENT

Scholars have connected the Mandaean people with the religions of Christianity, Manichaeism, Mithraism, and Zoroastrianism.[19] There are commonalities with the Persian religion of Zurvan Arkana.[20] The Yale Semitist, Julian Obermann, in his discussion of Aramaic incantation bowls, finds elements of "Chaldean witchcraft and astrology... Iranian eschatology and demonology... (and) Jewish monotheism."[21] The early

---

[19] Edwin M. Yamauchi, *Pre-Christian Gnosticism: A Survey of the Proposed Evidences* (Grand Rapids, MI: William B. Eerdmans Publishing Company, 1973), xvi.

[20] Svend Aage Pallis, *Mandaean Studies*, 2nd ed. (Amsterdam: Philo Press, 1926), 69, 72.

[21] Julian Obermann, "Two Magic Bowls: New Incantation Texts from Mesopotamia," *The American Journal of Semitic Languages and Literatures* 57, no. 1 (January 1, 1940): 29.

Muslim writers conflated the terms Sabian (*Sabi'un*) and Nabatean for any pagan cult.[22] For example, as late as the 1950s a westerner living in Southern Iraq reported that all uncircumcised men at that time were derisively called Sabian, regardless of religion or ethnicity.[23] The Russian orientalist Daniel Chwolson (1818–1911) made a connection between the Mandaeans and the Elchasaites[24] based on Arabic and Persian references.[25] The explanation for this mélange is given by the twentieth century Jewish historian and Hebrew scholar Yehezkel Kaufmann, who wrote, "We designate as pagan all the religions of mankind from the beginnings of recorded history to the present, excepting Israelite religion and its derivatives, Christianity, and Islam."[26]

Dr. Şinasi Gündüz, a scholar of comparative religions from Samsun University in Turkey, is exceptional among academics in arguing that the Mandaeans did not worship the planets. Gündüz takes the exclusionary position that the

---

[22] Jaakko Hämeen-Anttila, *The Last Pagans of Iraq: Ibn Waḥshiyya And His Nabatean Agriculture* (Leiden: Brill, 2006), 37.

[23] Wilfred Thesiger, *Marsh Arabs* (London: Penguin Books, 1967), 127.

[24] Also spelled *Elkasaites* or *Helkesaites*. See The Catholic Encyclopedia entry, *"Elcesaites"* http://www.newadvent.org/cathen/05372a.htm, accessed 1/25/2012. See Hastings' *Encyclopaedia of Religion and Ethics*, entry *"Elkesaites"* Vol. 9, 262-9.

[25] Şinasi Gündüz, *The Knowledge of Life: The Origins and Early History of the Mandaeans and Their Relations to the Sabians of the Qur'an and to the Harranians* (Oxford University Press, 1994), 5.

[26] Jonathan Elukin, "Maimonides and the Rise and Fall of the Sabians: Explaining Mosaic Laws and the Limits of Scholarship," *Journal of the History of Ideas* 63, no. 4 (October 2002): 637. Citing Kaufmann, The Religion of Israel, trans. Moshe Greenberg (Chicago, 1969), 21.

Mandaeans believed the planets to be wholly evil.[27] Yet culturally, there is no question that the Mandaeans do use astrology and do practice a form of astral religion.[28] The archeologist W. Stewart McCullough (Canadian, 1902–1982) refers to the Mandaean priests as "the community's astrologers," and continues, "For the Mandaeans believe that the stars and the planets are under the control of the King of the Light, and that the lives of men are in some way influenced by the heavenly bodies."[29]

In 1949, Geo Widengren (1907–1996) found similarities between Mandaean writings and the literature of Manichaeism and the early Syrian Christian Church.[30] There is agreement that some Manichaean hymns are translations of Mandaean poems.[31] There is a debate whether the Prophet Mani was actually raised in a Mandaean community.[32] However,

---

[27] Gündüz, *The Knowledge of Life*, 206, 221, 222, 236.

[28] E. S. Drower, *Diwan Abatur, or Progress Through the Purgatories* (Vatican City: Biblioteca Apostolica Vaticana, 1950), iv; E. S. Drower, *The Mandaeans of Iraq and Iran: Their Cults, Customs, Magic, Legends, and Folklore*, 1st ed. (Oxford: Clarendon Press, 1937), 74–99, 104; Pallis, *Mandaean Studies*, 19–22, 37–40, 210. ; Gertrude Bell, *Arab War Lords and Iraqi Star Gazers: Gertrude Bell's The Arab of Mesopotamia*, ed. Paul Rich, 2nd ed. (Lincoln, NE: Authors Choice Press, 2001), 94. etc.

[29] W.S. McCullough, *Jewish and Mandaean Incantation Bowls in the Royal Ontario Museum* (Toronto, Canada: University of Toronto Press, 1967), xvi.

[30] Geo Widengren, *Mesopotamian Elements in Manichaeism, Studies in Manichaean, Mandaean, and Syrian-gnostic Religion* (King and Saviour Seris No. 2) (Uppsala: Lundequistska bokhandeln, 1946).

[31] Buckley, *GSS*, 18. Buckley credits Torgny Säve–Söderbergh Studies (1949) with this discovery.

[32] Albert Henrichs, "Mani and the Babylonian Baptists: A Historical Confrontation," *Harvard Studies in Classical Philology* 77 (1973): 23–59.

since the discovery of the Cologne Mani Codex in 1969, there is agreement that he was a practicing member of a Baptist community living in the southern part of Mesopotamia before founding the religion that bears his name.[33] In this debate, the Harvard historian Albert Henrichs makes an astute observation about religious classifications: "The existing code names are not unambiguous, and they are subject to misuse."[34] The Mandaeans themselves were adept at adopting and manipulating "code names" for their own benefit and survival. This skill is not unnoticed even among them, and a modern Mandaean is quoted saying, "Well, we were Muslims, reading the Qur'an. Now we're Jewish, reading the Bible!"[35]

The tribal groups living in the Tigris–Euphrates marshlands are generically called the Marsh Arabs, in Arabic *Ma'dan*.[36] The Mandaeans are in fact a distinct tribal group within the mostly Shi'a tribes that make up the Marsh Arabs. Communities that practice the Mandaean religion are also called Mandaeans.[37] In general we can with confidence say that the Mandaeans are a Gnostic sect that resides in the Persian Gulf area, and that they are a distinct ethnic community or tribe in the region.

The Mandaic scholar Edmondo Lupieri (Italian, b. 1950) holds the Cody Chair of Theology at Loyola University and is a leading Mandaean scholar. He describes Mandaeanism as "...an esoteric religious knowledge, reserved for a chosen few and preserved through centuries of adversity...(and) a com-

---

[33] Albert Henrichs, "The Cologne Mani Codex Reconsidered," *Harvard Studies in Classical Philology* 83 (1979): 339–367.

[34] Ibid., 357.

[35] Buckley, *MAT*, 123.

[36] Thesiger, *Marsh Arabs*, 30, 92.

[37] Lupieri, *TLG*, xix, 5.

munity of believers with a minimum of theological ideas."[38]
He believes that Mandaeans have been able to survive because their limited theology has permitted them to adapt to
changing social conditions over the years. Another prominent
Mandaic scholar, Jorunn Jacobsen Buckley, who has worked
extensively with Mandaean literature and is an advocate for
Mandaean refugees, adds, "Early on, the religion clearly expe-
riences more or less hostile contacts with various forms of
Christianity and becomes acquainted with Babylonian rem-
nants, Zoroastrianism, Manichaeism, and other religions."[39]

The most celebrated Mandaean scholar is E.S. Drower
(British, 1879–1972, see section 1.2.). She proposed that at
the time of their emigration to Southern Mesopotamia, the
Mandaeans had "no preference to religion," but took on elements of Mazdaism and Zoroastrianism.[40] Drower was open
to new evidence, and in 1962 she wrote that early Mandaeanism "was originally a sect which flourished in Judaea and Sa-
maria, then possibly in Parthian–Jewish settlements and in
Transjordania, and that it was a hybrid strongly influenced by
Magianism and Jewish gnosticism."[41] While her emphasis on
Hebrew influence replaced her earlier preference for a Persian
influence, she still believed that "The Mandaean or Nasoraean
religion is a system with no definite theology. It is, and apparently was from the first, an elaborate system of symbolical
rites, meticulously preserved and performed by an hereditary
priesthood."[42] Like Hinduism, the cult was preserved by the

---

[38] Ibid., xviii–xix.

[39] Buckley, *MAT*, 3.

[40] Drower, *MII*, 10.

[41] E. S. Drower, "Mandaean Polemic," *Bulletin of the School of Oriental and African Studies*, University of London 25, no. 1/3 (January 1, 1962): 448.

[42] Ibid., 438.

priesthood, but unlike Hinduism, Mandaeanism at no time was endorsed by a royal family or dynasty. As Drower points out, "**Naṣiruta** (in its lay form Mandaeanism, **Mandtaiuta**) never became a state religion."[43]

The study of Mandaeans often uses the rubric of Gnosticism, and this is appropriate and correct. In 1867 Julius Petermann (German, 1801–1876) published a facsimile of the *Ginzā*,[44] which in his preface he calls "a most remarkable work of the Mandaeans…of both the highest importance and the greatest size."[45] Only one hundred copies of the Mandaic facsimile were printed. Gorgias Press reprinted the work in 2007 with a new introduction by Professor Charles Häberl of Rutgers University. He writes, "Despite the fact that the Mandaeans are the only Gnostic sect to survive from the period in which these sects first emerged, and the fact that the *Ginzā* is the only Gnostic scripture in current use by any religious community, following an unbroken tradition from late antiquity, the *Ginzā* continues to be one of the most inaccessible works of world literature."[46] The survival of Mandaean literature, including the astrological *Sfar Malwaśia*, is remarkable given the rarity of the books; however, the inaccessibility of the literature is equivalent to the inaccessibility of the people themselves.

---

[43] Ibid.

[44] **Ginzā** is translated as "collection," "treasury." or "library." The *Ginzā* is also called **siddra rabba**, or "great book" and incorrectly as *The Book of Adam*. It is composed of two parts referred to as the *Right Ginzā* (GR) and the *Left Ginzā* (GL). There are German (1867) and Arabic (2001) translations of the *Ginzā*. There is no English translation at this time.

[45] Julius Petermann, The Great Treasure or Great Book, Commonly Called "*The Book of Adam*," *The Ginzā*, ed. Charles Häberl (Piscataway, NJ: Gorgias Press, 2007), 1.

[46] Ibid., Häberl's Introduction, vii.

The British explorer and political officer Gertrude Bell (1868–1926) perhaps said it best without referencing religion at all: "A curious phenomenon in Mesopotamia is the existence of a mass of people who have borrowed from all the races about them and have adopted customs belong to all, and yet are totally isolated from them socially."[47] Regardless of the notions and ideas of the scholars, this community self–identifies themselves as Mandaean.[48]

The Mandaeans have preserved their literature through hand–made copies and not in an oral tradition. They believe their language and alphabet are sacred.[49] Drower writes, "Few laymen could, or can, read or write Mandaean; literacy is mostly confined to the priestly class."[50] Even though most Mandaeans cannot read the Mandaic language, wealthy families keep copies of books—that they cannot read—as a sign of devotion and status.[51] Much like Sanskrit or other sacred languages, Mandaic was a tongue preserved by the educated elite; a **shganda** (acolyte) began learning the **abage** (alphabet) at age four and became known as a **yalufa** upon achieving literacy.[52] (A **yalufa** is skillful enough to make amulets, recite

---

[47] Bell, *Arab War Lords and Iraqi Star Gazers*, 94.

[48] "The Mandaeans are part of the indigenous people of Iraq. They are a religious and ethnic minority that is facing annihilation." Mandaean Associations Union, http://www.mandaeanunion.org. Accessed 7/1/11, and 11/28/11.

[49] Drower, *MII*, 240. The alphabet or "abage" is described 240–4; Lynn Thorndike, *A History of Magic and Experimental Science, Vol. 1* (New York: Columbia University Press, 1929), 450,n.1.

[50] Drower, *MII*, 20.

[51] Petermann, *The Ginzā*, vii. Professor Häberl notes, "...copying the *Ginzā* was meritorious not only for the priest who copied it but also for the person who commissioned the copy."; Buckley, *GSS*, 2.

[52] Drower, *MII*, 146.

prayers, or consult the *Sfar Malwaśia.*) The catalog of Mandaic works is principally religious. The exceptions are magical and apotropaic, such as incantation bowls[53] and talismans.[54]

1.2. THE TRANSLATOR, LADY DROWER

Ethel May Stefana (nee Stevens) Drower, born December 1, 1879, died January 27, 1972, is known for her anthropological studies in Iraq, and as the expert in the literature, history, and religion of the *Subba* or Mandaeans.[55] No study of the Mandaeans is possible without recognizing her contributions to the field.[56] One historian wrote, "Lady Drower has won the gratitude of all scholars interested in Mandaic studies by her assiduous preoccupation with the publication of the texts that she collected in her many years of contact with the Mandaeans."[57] Her personal collection of manuscripts, now entrusted

[53] Michael G. Morony, "Magic and Society in Late Sasanian Iraq," in *Prayer, Magic, and the Stars in the Ancient and Late Antique World*, ed. Scott Noegel, Joel Walker, and Brannon Wheeler (University Park, PA: Pennsylvania State University Press, 2003), An example of the current research on incantation bowls.

[54] Edwin M. Yamauchi, *Mandaic Incantation Texts* (Piscataway, NJ: Gorgias Press, 2005); McCullough, *Jewish and Mandaean Incantation Bowls in the Royal Ontario Museum*; James A Montgomery, *Aramaic Incantation Texts from Nippur* (Philadelphia: University of Pennsylvania Museum, 1913), There is extensive scholarship on the "magic bowls" and these books are a partial representation.

[55] J. B. Segal, "Obituary: Ethel Stefana, Lady Drower (1 December 1879-27 January 1972)," *Bulletin of the School of Oriental and African Studies*, 35, no. 3 (1972): 621–622.

[56] Yamauchi, "The Present Status of Mandaean Studies," 90.

[57] Jonas C. Greenfield, "Review: A Pair of Nasoraean Commentaries. Translated by E. S. Drower," *Journal of the American Oriental Society* 90, no. 2 (April 1, 1970): 339–340.

to the Bodleian Library at Oxford, is given the catalog descriptor DC for Drower Collection.[58] Drower and Rudolf Macuch collaborated to compile *A Mandaic Dictionary* in 1963.[59]

Drower began her career in 1909, writing romance novels that were often placed in the exotic Near East.[60] She married Edwin Drower in 1910, becoming the Lady Drower when he was knighted. The couple moved to Iraq, where Sir Drower was stationed from 1921–1946. There Lady Drower took to exploring the local environs, and like Gertrude Bell before her, charmed and befriended many otherwise hostile natives.[61] Lady Drower's first non–fiction work was *The Mandaeans of Iraq and Iran: Their Cults, Customs, Magic, Legends, and Folklore*, published in 1937. This and all of her future publications were under the name E.S. Drower. She is occasionally referenced as Lady Drower when cited in scholarly work. Buckley has edited and published Drower's letters, which are a major contribution to Mandaean studies.[62]

---

[58] Lupieri, *TLG*, 54–59; Buckley, *GSS*, Appendix C "The Drower Collection."

[59] E. S Drower and R Macuch, *A Mandaic Dictionary* (Oxford: Clarendon Press, 1963).

[60] For example, *Cedars, Saints and Sinners in Syria*, published in 1926 under the name E.S. Stevens.

[61] Segal, "Obituary: Ethel Stefana, Lady Drower (1 December 1879-27 January 1972)."

[62] E. S. Drower, *Lady E. S. Drower's Scholarly Correspondence: An Intrepid English Autodidact in Iraq*, ed. Jorunn Jacobsen Buckley, Numen Book Series 137 (Leiden: Brill, 2012), Chapter 1 covers the *Sfar Malwašia*, including her extensive correspondence with Cyrus Gordon.

1.3. HISTORICAL EVIDENCE

Divergent theories about the geographical origin of the Man-daeans have been favored at various times.[63] Lupieri has com-posed a thorough chronological history of all the scholarly evidence and theories in his book, *The Mandaeans: The Last Gnostics*. Another excellent source is Japanese–American histo-rian Edwin M. Yamauchi's work *Pre–Christian Gnosticism*.[64] His work is organized by cultural and religious themes, such as Hermetic, Syriac, Coptic, Jewish, etc., and identifies the chal-lenges of evaluating the material from these perspectives.

The primary question is: Did the Mandaeans come from the East and have a Persian/Zoroastrian lineage, or did they come from the West and have a Palestinian–Jewish–Christian paternity?[65] There are many proposals, including one mytho-logical story from the Mandaeans themselves, which place their homeland in Ceylon, the modern day Sri Lanka.[66] Based on work by Buckley, Lupieri believes that the first scribe of the sacred texts was a man named Zazai, active at the end of the Parthian Empire (247 BCE–224 CE).[67] Buckley used col-ophons[68] to construct a 'family tree' of Mandaean copyists in her book *The Great Stem of Souls*. According to Buckley, the Mandaeans are the first historical Gnostic sect and proposes an origin date of c. 270 CE.[69] She writes, "The presence of

[63] Müller-Kessler, "The Mandaeans and the Question of Their Origin," 48.

[64] Yamauchi, *Pre-Christian Gnosticism*, [entire].

[65] Buckley, *GSS*, A concise history of the players and their positions in the debate, 297–339.

[66] Drower, *MII*, 10; Lupieri, *TLG*, 129.

[67] Lupieri, *TLG*, 169–171.

[68] Colophon: the list of scribes beginning with the current copyist going back to the first recorded one.

[69] Buckley, *GSS*, 339.

Zazai in the 270s indicates the existence of a fully developed Mandaean religion at that time."[70]

The first textual historical reference to the Mandaeans comes from tenth–century Baghdad, in Ibn al–Nadim's *Fihrist*.[71] In Chapter Nine of the *Fihrist*, the different Sabian sects are listed, including the Manichaeans and the Syrian–Christian Marconites.[72] One sect is described as living in the swamps of the Euphrates and called al–Mughtasila[73], meaning 'those who wash themselves.'[74] The *Fihrist* provides the additional information that "…(The Mughtasila) agreed with the Manichaeans about the two elemental [principles], but later their sect became separated. *Until this our own day, some of them venerate the stars*."[75] (My emphasis.) Chapter Eight of the *Fihrist* should also be cited, because it deals with exorcists, jugglers, and magicians: "One group of philosophers and servants of the stars assert that they have talismans, based on [astronomical] observations."[76] The *Sfar Malwašia* has several chapters on talismans, most of them with some astrological basis, e.g., "The sign of Aries, write for him, 'I came, and not alone,'

---

[70] Jorunn Jacobsen Buckley, "The Colophons in the Canonical Prayerbook of the Mandaeans," *Journal of Near Eastern Studies* 51, no. 1 (January 1992): 34.

[71] Also written *"The Fihrist"* or *"Ketab al-Fehrest."* Composed in 987 CE by Abu'l-Faraj Muhammad bin Is'hāq al-Nadim (d. 995 CE).

[72] al-Nadim, *The Fihrist, Two Volumes*, trans. Bayard Dodge, 1st ed. (New York: Columbia University Press, 1970), Chapter 9, 745–825.

[73] Ibid., 811. The sect becomes known as Sabat al–bata'ih, or "the Sabians of the Marsh."

[74] James Hastings, *Encyclopaedia of Religion and Ethics* (Edinburgh: T. & T. Clark, 1908), vols. 9, 268.

[75] al-Nadim, FAN, 811.

[76] Ibid., 726.

which is written [on the talisman] at dusk."[77] The Nabataean magician Ibn Waḥshīya al–Kaldānī is documented in the *Fihrist*.[78] He may have a connection with the Mandaeans[79], and wrote a book on astrology. Another source of valuable information is the gifted writer and polyglot al–Bīrūnī (973–1051).[80]

The next historical reference comes in 1555, when Portuguese Jesuits in Basra reported discovery of a group they called the "Saint John Christians" living in the area of Hormuz.[81] They recognized various aspects of the Mandaean cult, particularly baptism and a practice that looked like the Eucharist, and concluded that these people must be lost descendants of the followers of John the Baptist. The Catholic Encyclopedia lists 'Mandaean' as an equivalent name for the Nasoraeans, Sabians, and Christians of St. John, although the last is now disavowed—"The name 'Christians of St. John' is of European origin and based on a mistake."[82] But in the six-

---

[77] Drower, *SM*, 93.

[78] al-Nadim, FAN, 731.

[79] Gündüz, *The Knowledge of Life*, 119. "Since the Mandaeans (or proto–Mandaeans) probably had some kind of contact with the Nabataeans in Palestine..."

[80] Helaine Selin, ed., *Encyclopaedia of the History of Science, Technology, and Medicine in Non-Westen Cultures*, 1st ed. (Boston, MA: Kluwer Academic, 1997), Entry "Al–Bīrūnī" (Abū al–Rayḥān Muḥammad ibn Aḥmad al–Bīrūnī) 157–158; al-Bīrūnī, *The Chronology of Ancient Nations*, trans. C. Edward Sachau (London: William H. Allen and Co., 1879); al-Bīrūnī, *BOI*.

[81] Lupieri, *TLG*, This section is based on Lupieri, Chapter 2, "The Mandaeans and the West."

[82] Arendzen, J. (1911). Entry: 'Nasoræans' The Catholic Encyclopedia. New York: Robert Appleton Company. Retrieved November 28, 2011 from New Advent: http://www.newadvent.org/cathen/10705a.htm.

teenth century it was a plausible and useful idea for all parties concerned. The missionaries received funding from Rome, military protection from Lisbon, and began converting the Mandaeans to Catholicism.[83] The Portuguese drew upon their missionary experience with the Saint Thomas Christians of Kerala, India, another group of "lost Christians" ripe for re–conversion. The Mandaeans apparently knew about the missionary work in India, and there are records of Mandaean boys from Hormuz being sent to the Jesuit College at Goa.[84] The schoolboys returned to the Persian Gulf well–versed in the appropriate religious, political, and economic jargons of the time, as well as being fluent in Portuguese.

Many Mandaeans received Catholic baptism during this time; however, suspicions were raised several decades later, when a new Catholic order took control of the region. A review of the missionary records by the Carmelites showed hundreds of baptisms in the Basra region, but no Christian marriages or funerals. The Portuguese had apparently been duped by the Mandaeans.[85]

---

[83] The Mandaeans at this time were persecuted by the Turkish administrators who controlled the region for the Ottoman Empire which was actively expanding into Europe and Northern Africa. It is hypothetical, but the Mandaeans may have been used by the Europeans as spies or agents of counter-intelligence against the Ottomans.

[84] Lupieri, *TLG*, 70.

[85] Lupieri's account includes the Mandaeans pretending to be Christians, St. John Christians, Chaldean Christians, converted Mandaeans becoming mercenary fighters for the Portuguese, and relocation of converted Mandaeans to India and Sri Lanka. They presented their own "Bishop" even though he was of the Orthodox church, to claim Christian protection, all while still practicing "pagan" rituals. Lupieri describes the cross purposes of the missionaries in the field and the authorities in Rome, the pressures of colonialism and war. The Mandaeans, until recently,

The Mandaeans have been confused with many other groups over their history, including the fourth-century Nasaraean sect.[86] The "cultural elites" of the Mandaeans are called the **naṣuraiia** or **naṣiruta**.[87] These were the people who had received direct experience with the Divine Light; the common people were called **mandaiia**. The term **naṣiruta** sounded similar to the words 'nazorean' or 'nazarene,' and that was enough to allow the Mandaeans to pass as members of the fourth–century Jewish–Christian sect with followers spread from Palestine to India. Similarly, the name of the village leader in Mandaic is **ris ama,** which sounds like *rabba* or *rabbi* if trading with a Jew.[88] The term *rabiānum* was used to address the local leader in the early Old Babylonia period (twentieth —sixteenth centuries BC).[89] Widengren is more explicit in connecting the Akkadian *rabi–miksu,* meaning chief customer, with the Sumerian ideogram MASKIM and *rabiṣu* meaning both customer and gate–keeper.[90] The Mandaean calendar uses twelve months and five intercalary days called the **Parwanaia/Paruanaiia, Panja/Panǧa.**[91] Gordon calls attention to the apparent use of the Egyptian calendar and finds

---

have shown themselves to be adept at taking advantage of chaos created when the goals of political and religious power conflict.

[86] Gündüz, *The Knowledge of Life*, 109–10, 114.

[87] Lupieri, *TLG*, 9.

[88] Ibid., 11.

[89] Marten Stol, "Review: Local Power in Old Babylonian Mesopotamia by Andrea Seri," *Journal of the American Oriental Society* 127, no. 2 (April 1, 2007): 212.

[90] Widengren, *Mesopotamian Elements in Manichaeism*, 93.

[91] Drower, *MII*, 83; Lupieri, *TLG*, 19.

this evidence of a Coptic connection.[92] Häberl, in comparison, chooses this as evidence of the use of the Sassanian calendar.[93] The Mandaean **Panja** is compared to the Persian festival of the same name. [94] The Sanskrit word for five is *panchā*, which is the name of the Hindu almanac, *panchānga*, meaning 'five limbs.' These points establish how malleable the identity of the Mandaeans is, and also to illustrate the geographic and cultural range of their historical contacts.

The Mandaeans predate Muhammad and there has never been any confusion that Mandaeans could be Muslims.[95] At best, they were a pagan tribe to be converted to Islam. However, they did claim protection under Qur'anic law as Sabians, just as the Harranians in the north had done.[96] Widengren proposes that there were two branches of Manichaeism, one to the north that became associated with Harran, and one to the south that was associated with the Sabians.[97] This is not possible because, as we have shown, the Mandaeans predate or are contemporary to the Prophet Mani. Yet the idea of gnostic communities migrating north and south is sound. The confusion of the marsh–dwelling Sabians and the *Sabi* tribe

---

[92] Cyrus H. Gordon, "Review: Handbook of Classical and Modern Mandaic by Rudolf Macuch," *Journal of Near Eastern Studies* 26, no. 2 (April 1, 1967): 134–5.

[93] Häberl, "Review of Das Mandäische Fest Der Schalttage by Bogdan Burtea Review," 208.

[94] S. H. Taqizadeh, "An Ancient Persian Practice Preserved by a Non-Iranian People," *Bulletin of the School of Oriental Studies*, University of London 9, no. 3 (January 1, 1938): 608.

[95] Occasionally an older text on Gnosticism will conflate Mandaeans with Islam, but this is patently incorrect.

[96] T. M. Green, *The City of the Moon God: Religious Traditions of Harran* (Leiden: Brill, 1997), 2–4.

[97] Widengren, *Mesopotamian Elements in Manichaeism*, 176–179.

of Yemen is yet another hypothetical explanation for the inclusion of Sabeans in the Qur'an.[98] For researchers of the history of astrology, it is enough to know that people calling themselves Harranians[99] and Sabians were both known to include astral worship in their cult activities, and both were able to survive under Muslim rule by claiming to be people mentioned in the Qur'an.[100]

The Mandaean homeland is the marshy area in the low plains of Iran and Iraq, primarily around the waterway formed by the confluence of the Tigris and Euphrates rivers, called the *Shatt al-Arab*. Mandaeans historically are craftsmen known for their distinctive gold and silver work, and as skilled boat builders.[101] Both of these professions encouraged contact with people outside of the Mandaean faith; Muslims sought out the Mandaeans for their jewelry, and boat building was a major industry in the Persian Gulf.[102] The Mandaeans

---

[98] Lupieri, *TLG*, 66–7, 67fn9.

[99] Ibid., 85, 85fn48.

[100] There are two ways for people to claim protected status from the Qur'an. The first is simply to prove that because your community name is written in the Qur'an it means that God created that community and merits protection. The second is to claim that you have a "sacred text" that was divinely revealed. This approach denies inclusion in the Qur'an, but finds endorsement as a prophetic religion.

[101] Lupieri, *The Mandaeans*, 6; Aprim, Frederick, "Mandaeans: The True Descendents of Ancient Babylonians and Chaldeans." ©2003-4. Mandaean Associations Union. http://www.mandaeanunion.org/History/EN_History_009.htm. Accessed 1/25/2012.

[102] Drower, *MII*, 51; Bell, *Arab War Lords and Iraqi Star Gazers*, 95; Lupieri, *TLG*, 6; George F. Hourani and John Carswell, *Arab Seafaring: In the Indian Ocean in Ancient and Early Medieval Times*, Expanded ed. (Princeton University Press, 1995).

were exposed to many different variants of occidental and oriental culture through these livelihoods. As Lupieri points out, the area in which the Mandaeans lived in was always a "crossroads for the traffic connecting the Far East to the Middle East."[103]

Like the modern Parsis in India, the Mandaeans do not allow conversion into their faith.[104] Their language and holy books are read only by priests, an elite position that is acquired by heredity and exclusive training.[105] The religion was nearly extinguished in the 1830s during a cholera epidemic which killed most of the priestly families.[106] Two cousins, Yahia Bihram and Ram Zihrun were not ordained, but had been trained for the priesthood at the time of the epidemic. They receive credit and acknowledgement for rescuing and preserving the faith of the Mandaeans.[107]

The Mandaeans are a disenfranchised people whose culture survived for at least 1800 years by ingenuity, guile, and luck. Rudolf Macuch (1919–1993) was a leading Mandaic scholar in Berlin. Even though he worked with Drower, who conducted field research on the living Mandaeans, Macuch stated that the culture was already extinct, that "…the true **nasiruta** [Mandaeans] died in the 1831 cholera when the laypeople were compelled to take over the leadership."[108] The

---

[103] Lupieri, *TLG*, 131.

[104] Buckley, *MAT*, 123.

[105] Ibid., 98.

[106] Lupieri, *TLG*, 116.

[107] The devastation of the 1831 cholera epidemic and the heroic efforts to re-establish the Mandaean priesthood is covered by all the major Mandaean scholars. Buckley's treatment in *The Great Stem of Souls*, is particularly touching. (Ch. 7 "The Life of Yahia Bihram")

[108] Buckley, *GSS*, 308, citing Macuch, "Anfange der Mandaer." 163.

American invasion of Iraq and the First Persian Gulf War (1990–1991) could become the historical event that truly ends the Mandaeans as a living culture.[109] After the war, Saddam Hussein took punitive action against tribes that had helped the Americans ("In the early 1990s…Hussein ordered the marshes to be drained to punish the local population for an uprising after his failed invasion of Kuwait"[110]). The ethnic cleansing pogrom of Saddam Hussein resulted in the diaspora of many ethnic Iraqi groups. The Mandaeans were virtually unknown outside of the region until refugees began to be an issue in Western countries.[111] Western countries found it difficult to accommodate refugees from specific religious or ethnic backgrounds *en mass*. For example, a study done in Australia on the Mandaean refugees called for "Government immigration policy must prioritize the reunification of small, endangered groups to sustain cultural traditions."[112]

---

[109] Rory Stewart, *The Prince of the Marshes: And Other Occupational Hazards of a Year in Iraq* (Orlando. FL: Harcourt, 2006), 5–6.

[110] Juliette Jowit, "Paradise Found: Water and Life Return to Iraq's 'Garden of Eden'," The Guardian (UK, July 9, 2010), http://www.guardian.co.uk/world/2010/jul/09/iraq-marshes-reborn.

[111] Stewart, *The Prince of the Marshes*, 5–6; Chris Newmarker and Associated Press, "Mandaeans Ponder Their Survival.," *The Houston Chronicle*, February 10, 2007, http://www.chron.com/life/houston-belief/article/Mandaeans-ponder-their-survival-1629523.php. Russell Contreras and Associated Press, "UN: Iraqi Mandaeans Hard to Resettle in 1 Place," *Boston Globe*, November 11, 2011, http://www.boston.com/news/local/massachusetts/articles/2010/11/11/un_iraqi_mandaeans_hard_to_resettle_in_1_place/.

[112] Angela Nickerson et al., "Fear of Cultural Extinction and Psychopathology Among Mandaean Refugees: An Exploratory Path Analysis," *CNS Neuroscience & Therapeutics* 15, no. 3 (2009): Abstract.

In an April 2006 report, the Mandaean Human Rights Group provided this demographic information:

> Although it is very difficult to estimate, the Mandaeans could barely exceed fifty thousand at the present time. Their decreased numbers are due to continued persecution and forced mass conversions as well as relocation and assimilation. Currently they live in large cities such as Basra and Baghdad; very few remained in southern Iraqi cities like Umara and Nasiriya or southern Iranian cities like Ahwaz. During the past decade, and especially the past 3 years, thousands have escaped the dangerous political situation in Iraq, choosing self–exile and immigration. There are about 15000 Mandaean in different parts of Europe, 1500 in the United States, 1000 in Canada and about 4000 in Australia. There is also a large refugee population in various other countries: 950 families in Syria, 400 families in Jordan, 50 individuals in Yemen and 20 in Indonesia.[113]

Considered to be ethnically extinct in Iraq, the Mandaeans are a threatened population in Iran.[114] The Christian Joshua

---

[113] The Mandaean Union.

http://www.mandaeanunion.org/HMRG/EN_HMRG_011.html. Accessed 11/27/2011. The distinction made in this report between individuals and families emphasizes the importance of access to other Mandaean populations to find suitable marriage partners.

[114] "Mandaean Human Rights Annual Report" (Mandaean Human Rights Group, September 2011),
http://www.mandaeanunion.org/HMRG/MHRG Annual Report 2011.pdf.

Project lists 7,500 Mandaeans in Iran and 24,000 worldwide; however, they do not cite the sources for their information.[115] The worldwide population of Mandaeans is so few and so diffused as to be effectively unmeasurable; the Mandaeans have been scattered in the wind.

1.4. THE MANDAEAN PEOPLE AND THEIR RELIGION

The Mandaeans are both a religious sect and an ethnic culture.[116] Their name comes from the Aramaic word *manda* or *madda*, meaning 'knowledge' or in Greek, *gnosis*. Another possible etymology is **mandi**, the Mandaic word for their cult hut.[117]

The primary tenets of Mandaeanism are dualism, millennialism, spiritual rebirth—not reincarnation—requiring purity and the assistance of an intermediary spirit, and secrecy.[118] The German theologian Rudolf Bultmann (1884–1976) describes Gnosticism as a "synthetic phenomenon."[119] The sect incorporates practices that are variously identified as Christian

---

[115] The Joshua Project. http://www.joshuaproject.net/people-profile.php?peo3=13483&rog3=IR, accessed 11/27/2011.

[116] Lupieri, *TLG*, 5.

[117] Drower, *MII*, 10–13; Buckley, *GSS*, 367.

[118] Yuri Stoyanov, *The Other God: Dualist Religions from Antiquity to the Cathar Heresy* (London: Yale University Press, 2000), 124–5, for a brief discussion. These themes are repeated by Drower, Pallis, Lupieri, Buckley, and others.

[119] Rudolf Bultmann, *Primitive Christianity in Its Contemporary Setting*, trans. Reginald H. Fuller, (German Ed. 1949) 18th ed. (Philadelphia: Fortress Press, 1980), 162, see chapter IV "Gnosticism."

or Jewish.[120] Pre–Arab pagan rites are also found in the liturgy.[121] Like Hinduism and Buddhism, the Mandaeans integrate astral religion into their day–to–day observances.[122] This is most apparent in the practice of using private religious names based on the newborn's natal astrological chart.[123] To find the **malwaša**, or star–name, the priest calculates the chart and finds the appropriate name equating to the rising zodiacal sign at birth. The **malwaša** name is used in religious rites, and for medical diagnosis and treatment.[124]

The Mandaeans are, and have always been, a marginalized ethnic group. Their survival was contingent upon presenting the group as acceptable to the prominent authorities of any given time. This has resulted in a sort of chameleon effect[125] as the Mandaeans adapt to current conditions. The Mandaeans have a history for their people, though it is mythological and there are multiple versions: Drower records seven different cosmologies in the *Harwan Gawaita*.[126] Their writings are

---

[120] Drower, *MII*, xviii, 1; Buckley, *MAT*, xvii, 52; Yamauchi, *Pre-Christian Gnosticism*, 141, 160; Pallis, *Mandaean Studies*, 116–7.

[121] Yamauchi, "The Present Status of Mandaean Studies," 94; Taqizadeh, "An Ancient Persian Practice Preserved by a Non-Iranian People"; Lupieri, *TLG*, 28; Drower, *MII*, xx.

[122] Drower, *SM*, 1, 3; Drower, *Diwan Abatur, or Progress Through the Purgatories*, [entire]; Buckley, *MAT*, 41; Pallis, *Mandaean Studies*, 19–21.

[123] Lupieri, *TLG*, 17–18; Drower, *MII*, 26, 44, 60, 81–2; Buckley, *GSS*, 347; Drower, *SM*, 68–9.

[124] SF, 68-9. Buckley provides an updated list of the **malwaša**, or star-names in *GSS* 347-8.

[125] Lupieri, *TLG*, xvii.

[126] J. B. Segal, "Review: The Haran Gawaita and the Baptism of Hibil-Ziwa by E. S. Drower," *Bulletin of the School of Oriental and African Studies*, University of London 18, no. 2 (January 1, 1956): 373–375.

of a transitional period that is predominately post–Alexander and pre–Muhammad. Islamic rule resulted in further refinement of the "disguise" as certain aspects of the cult were promoted, such as baptism, while others were sublimated or hidden, such as astral worship. To outsiders, the Mandaeans appeared as another odd offshoot of the prominent Abrahamic religions. Internally, the Mandaeans believed they alone preserved the truth of **hiia mandaii**, "The Great Life."[127]

As noted, the Mandaeans are a Gnostic sect. Gnostic sects are inherently pessimistic, believing that the demiurge created the world as a mistake or at best under duress. The vagaries of Gnostic thought do not concern us here beyond the ideas of predetermination and fatalism, which foster a belief in astrology.

Predeterminism is a helpful philosophy for any disenfranchised group. The Mandaeans never had a "king of kings" living in a stone palace, nor a high priest tending a great temple. The survival of the Mandaeans required a submissive attitude in their political environment. Yet the practice of astrology demonstrates the importance of individual action and the belief that knowing fate is useful and that fate can somehow be modified. Of greater importance to the Mandaeans was living a life that would best prepare them for the ascent through the heavenly spheres after their physical death, and to successfully rejoin the "Life Immortal" in the spiritual world.[128] Astrology therefore participates in a mundane/practical and soteriological/ redemptive manner in the day–to–day lives of the Mandaeans.

The quiet defiance of the Mandaeans is also seen in their particular form of millennialism. Millennial belief is usually

---

[127] Lupieri, *TLG*, 39, def. fn38.

[128] M. Annus, "Some Otherworldly Journeys in Mesopotamian, Jewish, Mandaean and Yezidi Traditions," in *Of God(s), Trees, Kings, and Scholars: Neo-assyrian and Related Studies in Honour of Simo Parpola* (Helsinki: Finnish Oriental Society, 2009), 315–26.

attributed to Zoroastrian or Persian influence. The twentieth–century British historian Nicholas Campion describes the Zoroastrian cosmological perception as a "...view of the material world as a theatre of war in which good, represented by the god of light...was engaged in a perpetual struggle with evil in the form of the god of darkness," and maintains that this "struggle between opposing forces divided history into a succession of distinct periods."[129] The Mandaean cosmology shares this view, although the struggle between light and darkness takes place more often in the heavenly spheres than in our sub–lunar world. The exception is during the New Year Festival, when the powers of evil are manifest in the physical world. (New year festivals are addressed in sections 3.4-3.6.) The millennialism of the Mandaeans incorporates Semitic elements similar to those found in the writings of the Old Testament prophets. The constant struggle between good and evil is replaced with the ideas of a chosen people who suffer exile but in return gain prophecy and the promise of a messiah.[130]

1.5. GNOSTICISM

Even Mandaean scholars introduce their subject generically as the "...last living Gnostics. Their name, from the word *manda*, means 'Knowers.'"[131] The difficulty is that the term 'gnostic' is

---

[129] Nicholas Campion, *Dawn of Astrology: A Cultural History of Western Astrology Volume One* (London: Continuum, 2008), 77.

[130] Cyrus H. Gordon, *Before the Bible: The Common Background of Greek and Hebrew Civilisation* (London: Collins, 1962); Francis Legge, *Forerunners and Rivals of Christianity from 330 B.C. to 330 A.D.*, Two Volumes (Hyde Park, NY: University Books, 1964).

131 April D. DeConick, Professor of Biblical Studies, Rice University, from her website on Mandaeanism. http://www.aprildeconick.com/mandaeans.html. Accessed, 10/26/ 2011.

used indiscriminately, to the point that it is almost meaningless: The term must be qualified by epoch, culture, and language.[132] The *Sfar Malwaša* creates more challenges for gnostic researchers, because the Mandaeans are a historical people with a documented history and a living presence in our world. But the *Sfar Malwaša* is not included in the Mandaean religious canon.

The philosopher Hans Jonas (German, 1903–1993) published *The Gnostic Religion* in 1958, and it continues to be the most helpful text for attempting any kind of coherence in understanding the historical evidence of the Gnostics.[133] Jonas challenged the accepted assumption that Gnosticism was a development of Hellenistic culture.[134] He believed that the analysis of Coptic and Mandaean texts supported an oriental source such as Babylonia or Persia.[135] He proposed that the development of indigenous or traditional religion into a systematic theological system, that is, the transition between pagan and rational doctrines, required the admixture of both occidental and oriental thought.[136] He describes the "Hellenization of the East" and the "Orientalization of the West" as the synthesis that began with Alexander the Great and continued through to the Middle Ages.[137]

---

[132] Stoyanov, *The Other God*, 287; Hans Jonas, *The Gnostic Religion: The Message of the Alien God and the Beginnings of Christianity*, 2nd ed. enlarged. (Boston: Beacon Press, 1963), Preface to the 1st edition, xiii–xviii.

[133] Jonas, *The Gnostic Religion*.

[134] Bultmann, *Primitive Christianity in Its Contemporary Setting*, Ch. IV "Gnosticism" 162–171.

[135] Jonas, *The Gnostic Religion*, xv, xvi.

[136] Ibid., 17.

[137] For a discussion of gnostic and modern philosophies, see Jonas, *The Gnostic Religion*, Ch.13 "Epilogue: Gnosticism, Existentialism and Nihilism," 320-340.

The conflation of Gnosticism and astral religions is established through the archeological record, and particularly with the so–called Mystery Cults of the ancient world. Cumont believed that the stars were actively worshipped and that the qualities of the signs and planets were based on mythology and transferred to the calendar months: "…and their images figure in large numbers on the monuments of pagan worship, particularly on those of the mysteries of Mithra."[138]

Jonas respects the role astrology played in the Hellenization process: "In a one sided development of its original astral features, the older cult was transformed into an abstract doctrine, the reasoned system of astrology, which simply by the appeal of its thought–content, present in Greek form, became a powerful force in the Hellenistic world of ideas."[139] He complains that astrology has been misinterpreted as an "old" eastern wisdom, as in prehistoric and magical because of age. He believes what really is occurring is an original, new, and novel thought that synthesizes astral fatalism and stoicism, among other elements.[140]

The ephemeral nature of Gnosticism was noted by Irenaeus in *Against Heresies* (c. 180 CE). He complained, "Every day every one of them invents something new."[141] (Curiously, al–Bīrūnī makes the same complaint about the fecundity of Arabic parts in the post Gnostic, Islamic age.[142]) Lupieri compares Gnosticism in the Hellenistic culture to the explosion of new religions in the 1960's: "about seventy new Chris-

---

[138] Cumont, *Astrology and Religion Among the Greeks and Romans*, 66.

[139] Jonas, *The Gnostic Religion*, 16.

[140] Ibid., 21, 22, 24, 26.

[141] Ibid., 42, 178, cites Irenaeus, I.18.5.

[142] al-Bīrūnī, *BOI*, §476. Lists nearly 100 different Greek lots or Arabic parts which are a specialized astrological calculation, commenting, "they increase in number every day."

tian denominations were formed every day…and most of them in California."[143] The Warburg scholar Yuri Stoyanov uses the word "explosion" to describe this burst of spiritual creativity, but also says that the religions of ancient antiquity "…become increasingly difficult to discern and identify."[144] The plasticity of religion does not change with the *bricolage* of cultural influences over time. Campion says of the fifth century CE, "the religious climate in the late Roman Empire was complex and the relationship between Christianity and paganism defies simple categorization."[145]

The face of Gnosticism could change with the direction of the wind or the sun: From the east Gnosticism appeared Greek, but from the west Gnosticism was just pagan, and at noon it was incomprehensible to everyone. Jonas proposed a sort of litmus test for Gnostics by determining the onus of man's fall from grace: Abrahamic religions blamed Adam for the fall while Gnostic cults blamed the Archons [demiurge].[146]

Gnosticism is also confused with Hermeticism because both believe in the transformation of the soul.[147] Although Gnosticism as a singular religion is intangible, scholars appear content to classify the Mandaeans as Gnostic, whatever that is.[148] Caution is advised, however; as one reviewer of Jonas

---

[143] Lupieri, *TLG*, 33.

[144] Stoyanov, *The Other God*, 124.

[145] Nicholas Campion, "The Possible Survival of Babylonian Astrology in the Fifth Century CE: A Discussion of Historical Sources," in *Horoscopes and Public Spheres*, ed. Günther Oestmann, H. Darrel Rutkin, and Kocku von Stuckrad (Berlin: Walter de Gruyter, 2005), 69.

[146] Jonas, *The Gnostic Religion*, 307.

[147] Kevin Van Bladel, *The Arabic Hermes: From Pagan Sage to Prophet of Science* (Oxford University Press, 2009).

[148] Pagan and Gnostic are often used as equivalent terms in the primary material on Mandaeans.

writes, "Gnosticism presents an extraordinary challenge to a historian of ideas."[149]

The tendency of gnostic scholars has been to focus on the language and literature of the Mandaeans to establish connections between different heterodox cults, and their astrological literature has been mostly ignored.[150] This is unfortunate, because the astrological literature of the Mandaeans is such a good historical source for the evidence of how eastern and western cultures transmitted beliefs and customs, and this can help clarify different aspects of gnostic religions. Whereas the historical references to gnostic groups were written by detractors or apologists, for example Josephus or Augustine, the Mandaean literature is their own. The Mandaean literature is truly an original and primary source. The German researcher Christa Müller–Kessler observes that modern distinctions between literary and colloquial works are not accurate, and specifically names the *Sfar Malwaṧia* as a book not easily classified, saying it "belonged to the everyday life of the Mandaean community and other groups, and represented the intellectual knowledge of scribes and priests."[151]

In Mandaean cosmology, the creating demiurge is a masculine deity called **Ptahil**[152] who creates the feminine principle called **Ruha**. **Ruha** in turn creates "the Seven (planets) and the Twelve (zodiac signs)."[153] Astrology plays a major role in the Mandaean religious belief, as upon death the soul ascends

---

[149] Philip Merlan, "Review: Gnosis Und Spätantiker Geist by Hans Jonas," *The Journal of Philosophy* 55, no. 17 (1958): 743.

[150] Yamauchi, "The Present Status of Mandaean Studies," See also Buckley's note on scholarship, The Mandaeans, pp. 16–18. .

[151] Müller-Kessler, "The Mandaeans and the Question of Their Origin," 53, 54.

[152] Yamauchi, *MIT*, 63. He attributes Ptahil to the Egyptian creator god Ptah.

[153] *Ginzā* 1.27, 1.3, 11.2-3.

to heaven, passing through celestial portals or stations along the way.[154] The planets and zodiacal signs are considered evil because they harm via emotions: "Faults committed under planetary influences must be expiated after death."[155]

It is my conclusion that Mandaeanism is a pessimistic religion, and Lupieri agrees writing, "Ears to hear and eyes to see, this is the tragic ability of the Gnostics."[156] Jonas goes so far as to call Gnosticism a gentle form of nihilism.[157] Whereas modern nihilism is desperate because the world is indifferent—a true abyss—Gnostics like the Mandaeans find solace and perspective in negativity. There is human suffering, but it is minor when one looks beyond to see the universality of suffering.[158] There may be demonic forces in the world, but that just proves that there are divine forces as well. Most importantly, human beings are active agents, not passive instruments in the face of a cosmic scheme that is not a closed system. Jonas writes, "The dread and alienation and fear is challenged by the Messenger who delivers the message of hope, knowledge, transcendent God, and opens the path through the Spheres."[159]

---

[154] Compare to the Pythagorean Music of the Spheres, the Hermetic ascent and descent of the soul, Plato's Myth of Er, (*The Republic*, X.6) and Cicero's Dream of Scipio (*De re publica*, VI), etc.

[155] Yamauchi, *MIT*, 33.

[156] Lupieri, *TLG*, 35.

[157] Jonas, *The Gnostic Religion*, Epilogue, 320–338.

[158] Lupieri, *TLG*, 35.

[159] Jonas, *The Gnostic Religion*, 329.

1.6. JOHN THE BAPTIST AND BAPTISM

At some point in the development of their religious beliefs, the Mandaeans decided that Jesus was a false prophet, but that the man who baptized him was genuine. The Muslims accepted Jesus as a messenger or prophet, and the Mandaeans appear to have embraced John the Baptist sometime after the arrival of the Muslims in the Persian Gulf in 639 CE. We know this because the Mandaic word for John is **Iahia Iuhana**, which comes from the Arabic for John, *Yahya*.[160] (Islam is addressed in section 1.7.)

From about the sixteenth century CE onward, there are references to "Christians of Saint John" in the reports of European missionaries.[161] John the Baptist, not to be confused with the apostle St. John, is known for his austere lifestyle, his preaching about end–times, teaching repentance, performing the baptism of Jesus, and his martyrdom.[162]

Baptism, called **maṣbuta**, is the predominant ritual of the Mandaeans. They perform individual daily **maṣbutiata**, much like Hindus practice daily pujas (ritual offerings) at home, or the ritual washing of hands and feet before entering a mosque by Muslims. Special baptisms are conducted as needed after defilement, such as exposure to blood. There are also special baptisms that accompany rites of passage, illnesses, and as propitiations for good luck. The most elaborate baptisms are a community affair requiring the participation of priests, cer-

---

[160] Yamauchi, *Pre-Christian Gnosticism*, 124–5; Arthur E. Link, "The Earliest Chinese Account of the Compilation of the Tripiṭaka (II)," *Journal of the American Oriental Society* 81, no. 3 (1961): 96.

[161] Lupieri, *TLG*, 69, Ch.2 "The Mandaeans and the West."

[162] Mark 1.6:4-6, Matthew 3.4:1-3; Souvay, C. (1910). St. John the Baptist. In The Catholic Encyclopedia. New York: Robert Appleton Company. Retrieved November 20, 2011 from New Advent: http://www.newadvent.org/cathen/08486b.htm.

emonial objects, and ritual food. All **maṣbutiata** require the use of "running" or naturally moving water, which is called **jordana**.[163] Running water is "living water" and symbolically represents the celestial "River of Light" in the heavens.[164]

The ritual of baptism has a very profound meaning for the Mandaeans.[165] In the *Ginzā* is written, "Attire yourselves in white and cover yourselves with white which may correspond with the dazzling garments and raiments of Light."[166] **Jordana** is called the "garment of light" and the practice of baptism is meant to ritually reconnect the soul to the **almia d–nhura**, or the celestial worlds of light.[167]

1.7.   MANDAEANS AND ISLAM

As stated earlier, the Mandaeans existed in the pre–Islamic period.[168] Muhammad, living on the Arabian Peninsula, was not aware of the baptist sects living in the Persian Gulf region. It is likely that he did know about an indigenous tribe in Yemen known as the *Saba* or *Sheba*.[169] The Qur'an provides accommodation for existing sects and cults as part of the process of spreading the new religion of Allah. Acceptable

---

[163] Alternatively transliterated as **yardana, iardna**.

[164] Jonas, *The Gnostic Religion*, 97; Drower, *MII*, xxi; Lupieri, *TLG*, 13–14, 39; Gündüz, *The Knowledge of Life*, 111–2.

[165] Pallis, *Mandaean Studies*, 40–46, 162–167; Drower, *MII*, 100–123; Lupieri, *TLG*, 15–19.

[166] Pallis, *Mandaean Studies*, 166. GR I 25, 12–17.

[167] Lupieri, *TLG*, 39.

[168] Hämeen-Anttila, *The Last Pagans of Iraq*, See 1.4 "Continuity of pagn religious trandition in tenth–century Iraq." 46–52.

[169] Lupieri, *TLG*, 67; Agatharchides, *On the Erythraean Sea*, trans. Stanley M. Burstein (London: The Hakluyt Society, 1989), Book V §91, §99; 151, 159.

tribes, or potential converts, became known as *dhimmi*, or *al–Kitab*, meaning "people of the book."[170] This is not a reference to a tribe having a holy book; most Arabic tribes were illiterate. It has the literal meaning that these people are named in the holy book, the Qur'an:

> Sura 2:62 Indeed, those who believed and those who were Jews or Christians or Sabeans [before Prophet Muhammad] – those [among them] who believed in Allah and the Last Day and did righteousness – will have their reward with their Lord, and no fear will there be concerning them, nor will they grieve.[171]

The Mandaeans claim a lineage from Abraham who they called **Bahram**, "Yes, he was a Mandai, a Nasurai. His brother was *rish 'amma,* and they were a family of priests."[172] Therefore the Mandaeans are sometimes considered an Abrahamic religion; however, this classification is given because of their status as *dhimmi*. The Mandaeans do not practice circumcision, and priests are not allowed to cut their hair; any physical defect or injury is considered a sign of defilement.[173]

The only connection between the Muslims and the Mandaeans was the political reality of living in the same area. The Mandaeans recorded the arrival of the Muslims in their literature, which becomes an important date for Islamic historians. According to the *Haran Gawaita*, the "sons of the butcher"

---

[170]Qur'an, 29:46, 3:113-115, 2:62, 3:64, 22:17.

[171] Saheeh International, tran., *The Quran*, English. (Saheeh International, 1997).

[172] Drower, *MII*, 266. See section 1.3 for the definition of **"rish 'amma."**

[173] Ibid., 146–7.

entered Mesopotamia in 639 CE.[174] However, the Mandaean and Islamic religions share several tenets, such as revelation, prophets who provide holy scripture, end–times, and the duty to do good works. A prayer from the *Ginzā* instructs, "Be careful; make enquiry, display kindness, show compassion (during?) the homilies, and loose him from his sins. And Life is victorious."[175]

The Muslims may have protected Mandaeans in less direct methods than as *dhimmi*. The Finnish researcher Jaakko Hämeen–Anttila has translated the Nabatean works of Ibn Wahshiyya, and suggests that the intrusion of Islam actually helped the indigenous rural cultures. He writes, "Pagans stayed tied to their land while Muslim converts, at least partly, left for the cities. Thus, paganism had a fair chance to survive in the countryside where pagans were also permitted to practice their religion."[176]

1.8.   THE CONTENTS OF THE *SFAR MALWAŠIA*

The *Sfar Malwaša* consists of 289 pages of Mandaic which are translated into194 pages of English by Drower. The individual sections are numbered, although the first three sections are given distinct titles in the colophon: *The Book of the Signs of the Zodiac for Men*, *The Book of the Signs of the Zodiac for Women*, and the *The Book of Stars*. These first three sections concern individual horoscopy and extend for 66 pages. The material is based on zodiacal sign and house, and references the decans (three–part divisions of the signs) and planetary rulership by zodiacal sign. Only the visible planets and the Sun and the

---

[174] Lupieri, *TLG*, 166.

[175] *Ginzā*, Chapter 74 "The Letter"
http://www.essene.com/B%27nai-Amen/vhymns.htm, accessed 1/26/2012.

[176] Hämeen-Anttila, *The Last Pagans of Iraq*, 31.

Moon are used for prognostications. A short but very important section describes how the **malwaša**, or star–name for a child, is calculated. Although barely a page long, this section is critical evidence that the Mandaeans incorporated astrology and numerology into their religious and cultural practices. It also demonstrates the matrilineal naming convention of the Mandaeans. Drower makes the comment that the Mandaean star–names are rooted in Assyrian–Babylonian nomenclature.[177]

The next section, numbered Book IV, starts with a simple list of astrological terms such as the zodiacal signs, the names of the planets, the stars (planets) of the days of the week, the months that correspond to signs, the order of the spheres, the qualities of the signs and planets, the rulership, and the mean time it takes each planet to pass through a zodiacal sign. The information is given tersely and without comment. It is interesting that the names of the planets are the same deity names first given to the orbs by the Assyrians; for example, the Moon is called *Sin*, and Mercury is called *'Nbu*.[178] The brief astrological lesson is followed by a few fragments that have become inserted over time. (One deals with when to put on new clothes for the first time, another is about blood–letting.) Within the same book follow four pages of decumbiture calculations. The decumbiture is the astrological figure of the moment a person falls ill, and provides information about the diagnosis, progression, and prognosis of the disease. Infant mortality is predicted, as well as critical days for illnesses that begin on certain days and certain hours. The last portion is a list of prognostications for illness that start on particular days of the month, for example, "A person who falls ill on the seventh of the month up to twenty–one days, will recover and be cured."[179]

---

[177] Drower, *SM*, 69n14.

[178] Ibid., 70, 70n1.

[179] Ibid., 73.

Book V, called *The Book of the Moon,* is also concerned with decumbitures; however, this section gives prognostication for the day of the moon, not the civil day as in the previous section. "One who sickens on the seventh day of the moon, it will go hardly with him until the end of the month. If not then recovered, fear for him."[180] This is similar to Babylonian hemerologies that list auspicious and inauspicious days.[181]

Books VI and VII, twelve pages in the translation, contain charms against devils, lunacy–demons, and counter–spells.

Book VIII, *The Days of the Month,* is a sort of almanac or hemerology warning against actions taken on certain days, and recommending days for successful enterprises. For example, we are told that "the eighth of the month is good for boat–building."[182] The initial list of 30 days describes not lunar days, but calendar days. There is a portion at the end that actually does give prognostications based on the phase–days of the moon. It lists the light days of the month (1, 3, 9, 11, 13, 23, 26, and 28), which are favorable and auspicious. The dark days of the month (2, 4, 5, 7, 8, 24, 25, 27, 30) are considered evil. (Compare to the Babylonian "evil days" of 7, 14, 19, 21, and 28.[183])

Book IX concerns illnesses, and the result of illnesses that occur under different signs based on the eighth sign/house of where the illness begins. The number of sick days under each sign is given. Oddly, the number of children produced under each sign is also included in this section.

Book X contains much astrological information, although it begins with instructions on how to make the appropriate

---

[180] Ibid., 75.

[181] Erica Reiner, *Astral Magic in Babylonia* (Philadelphia: American Philosophical Society, 1995), 112.

[182] Drower, *SM,* 89.

[183] Reiner, *Astral Magic in Babylonia,* 113.

amulets for each sign of the zodiac.[184] Then follows the method of death for each sign, and a short section on the characteristics of the signs and houses. A fragment is inserted, interesting because it records when to approach a ruler: "Visit him when Mars is in Aries, (and) if the visit be on the third, or fourth, of the moon the visit will pass of smoothly."[185] More astrological information follows, such as the exaltation and depression of the planets including the nodes of the moon, the sextile aspect, the decans of the signs, the influence of the planets on a man, ending with a short list of considerations for choosing the day to perform certain activities.

Book XI continues with more directions on how to select days for certain activities. The activities are quite varied, e.g. cutting fingernails, entering partnerships, attending a musical concert, weaning a baby, buying and selling, etc.

Book XII is titled *The Opening of a Door,* and concerns geomancy.

Books XIII, XIV, XV, and XVI concern mundane predictions and are discussed in the last section of this paper.

Book XVII lists the geographical regions governed by the planets and the zodiac signs.

Book XVIII continues with mundane predictions, focusing on the day of the week the new year commences and the appearance of various meteorological phenomena such as winds and clouds. It includes predictions based on the observation of eclipses.

Book XIX discusses the transits of Saturn, halos of the sun, shooting stars and comets, and rainfall. Book XX discusses rainbows, earthquakes, extreme weather, "The Sword" (an atmospheric phenomenon), thunder, and other minor portents.

---

[184] Drower, *SM*, 93–4.

[185] Ibid., 95.

The *Sfar Malwašia* ends here, but additional material has been appended to the original text. Drower calls the next section Part II. Part II also contains information on various omens, yearly predictions, eclipses, and remedies. The last line before the colophon is, "And so this compilation from a Greek (*Rumia*) miscellany comprising calculations about the stars and horoscopes and information about what there is in the heavens according to days, months, and years, was compiled and completed."

1.9. THE ASTROLOGY IN THE *SFAR MALWAŠIA*

The scholarly assessment is that the *Sfar Malwašia* is a compilation of material from different sources, and from the previous description there is no reason to think otherwise. A chronological provenance of the astrological techniques should be possible. It is not enough to say, as the philosopher Robert Charles Zaehner (British, 1913–1974) has written, "Like the Zoroastrians, this extraordinary sect became familiar with astrology and astrolatry through their contact with Babylon."[186] There is much more to the story. At a minimum, a survey of the *Sfar Malwašia* reveals this level of astrological technique: a mature zodiacal system of twelve signs, the visible planets and the invisible lunar nodes, mundane houses, and timing techniques based on planetary periods.

The leading historian of mathematics was the philologist David E. Pingree (American, 1933–2005) of Brown University. (It is impossible to study the history of astrology without drawing upon Pingree's vast bibliography.) Pingree believes the basic features of astrology are established in the Western tradition by the Parthian period (247 BCE – 224 CE). The characteristics of astrology include "...a native's life influ-

---

[186] R. C. Zaehner, *Zurvan: A Zoroastrian Dilemma*, Reprint. (New York: Bibio and Tannen, 1955), 152.

enced by the individual zodiacal signs, the masculinization and feminization of the planets, and the planetary melothesia, and some traces of cararchic astrology dependent on the zodiacal sign occupied by the Moon."[187] The *Sfar Malwašia* includes hemerologies, lists of good and bad days for events and activities, in Books V and VIII.[188] These lists are not considered astrological by some scholars; however, they are similar to the system of hemerologies found in the Mesopotamian texts. [189]

Zodiacal constellations appear in the Babylonian MUL.APIN, composed in the seventh century BCE; however, the standard twelve–sign zodiac of equal divisions of arc does not appear until the fifth century BCE. By the Hellenistic period this standardized zodiac is known from Rome to Egypt, and from Persia to India.[190] The third century BCE is prominent in the history of astrology as the period when the Chaldean Berossus founded an astrological school on the Greek island of Cos, and wrote a history of Babylon. This is part of the classical record from Vitruvius:

> As for the branch of astronomy which concerns the influences of the twelve signs, the five stars, the sun, and the moon upon hu-

---

[187] David Pingree, *From Astral Omens to Astrology: From Babylon to Bīkāner* (Rome: Italiano per l'Africa e l'Oriente, 1997), 28.

[188] Drower, *SM*, 75–7, 88–92.

[189] Jacco Dieleman, "Stars and the Egyptian Priesthood," in *Prayer, Magic, and the Stars in the Ancient and Late Antique World*, ed. Scott Noegel, Joel Walker, and Brannon Wheeler (University Park, PA: Pennsylvania State University Press, 2003), 139n.9; Jeanette C. Fincke (Heidelberg), "The Babylonian Texts of Nineveh," *Archiv Für Orientforschung*, no. 50 (2004 2003): 133; Reiner, *Astral Magic in Babylonia*, 112–3.

[190] Robert Powell, *History of the Zodiac* (Sophia Academic Press, 2006), 203.

man life, we must leave all this to the calculations of the Chaldeans, to whom belongs the
art of casting nativities, which enables them
to declare the past and the future by means
of calculations based on the stars. These dis-
coveries have been transmitted by the men
of genius and great acuteness who sprang directly from the nation of the Chaldeans; first
of all, by Berossus, who settled in the island
state of Cos, and there opened a school.[191]

Timing techniques determine the time at which an event
will occur, or the period of life in which an event will happen.
The Hellenistic astrology Vettius Valens (120–175 CE) describes many elaborate timing techniques in Book Four of the
Anthology, including the division of life into time–periods, and
several methods for progressing the chart.[192] The Hellenistic
science writer Ptolemy (c. 90–169 CE) is the principal classical
source for timing in mundane astrology, using syzygies[193], especially those producing eclipses, and transits, particularly
ingresses, stations, and retrogrades.[194]

---

[191] Vitruvius, *The Ten Books on Architecture*, trans. Morris Hicky
Morgan (Cambridge, MA: Harvard University Press, 1914), 9.6.2,
http://www.gutenberg.org/files/20239/20239-h/29239-h.htm.

[192] Campion, *Dawn of Astrology: A Cultural History of Western Astrology
Volume One*, 216; James Herschel Holden, *A History of Horoscopic
Astrology*, 2nd ed. (Tempe, AZ: American Federation of
Astrologers, Inc., 1996), 50.

[193] Syzygies are the alignment of the sun, moon and earth producing
new and full moons, and eclipses. Astrologically these are also
known as the conjunction and opposition of the sun and moon.

[194] Ptolemy, *Tetrabiblos*, trans. F. E. Robbins, Loeb. (Cambridge, MA:
Harvard University Press, 1940), Book II.

At this point we must digress briefly to address the definition of 'historical astrology.' According to the astrologer Charles E. O. Carter (British, 1887–1968), there are three primary branches of astrology: genethlialogy or astrology pertaining to individuals, judicial or horary astrology, and the remainder of astrological techniques which fall under the heading of mundane astrology.[195] Within mundane astrology are found political astrology, astro–meteorology, the prediction of wars and famines, etc. In summary, Carter defines mundane astrology as "…all that concerned many people rather than a single person."[196] Campion makes a distinction between judicial and natural astrology, pointing out that similar to the different forms of Mesopotamian divination, one form is "provoked/operational" and the other form is "unprovoked/observational."[197] However, Pingree uses the term 'historical astrology' specifically in regard to the Persian or Sassanian technique of studying planetary conjunctions in relation to the rise and fall of political and religious institutions.[198] Pingree's translation of the eighth century Persian–Jewish astrologer Māshā'allāh on historical astrology is charming and precise: "…the pure prophecies and the dazzling miracles and what he judged about if for all these things…concerning judgments based on conjunctions and

---

[195] H. S. Green, Raphael, and Charles E. O. Carter, *Mundane Astrology: The Astrology of Nations and States* (New York: Astrology Center of America, 2005), 211.

[196] Ibid.

[197] Nicholas Campion, *The Great Year: Astrology, Millenarianism, and History in the Western Tradition*, First Printing. (London: Penguin, 1995), 262.

[198] E.S. Kennedy and David Pingree, *The Astrological History of Māshā'allāh*, First ed. (Cambridge, MA: Harvard University Press, 1971), vi.

world–year transfers (that is, vernal–equinox horoscopes)."[199] The rational is that the inception or birth chart of the world—or a dynasty or a religion—cannot be accurately determined; therefore, periods of time based on solar or seasonal cycles as well as longer planetary cycles are consulted for prognostications.[200] Therefore, 'historical astrology' as defined by Pingree is a subset of the mundane branch of astrology. (Mundane and political astrology as practiced by the Mandaeans are discussed in the third part of this study.)

According to Pingree, the techniques of 'historical astrology' are a development of the Sassanian period, and he finds much Sassanian material in the *Sfar Malwaša*.[201] He writes that by the Abbasid period, after 750 CE, the court astrologers "…were using a fully developed theory in which the conjunctions are linked to Iranian millennarianism and to the Indian theory of the Grand Conjunction at Aries 0° at the beginning of the Kaliyuga."[202] Pingree also notes that the beginning of the Indian Kali Yuga was equivalent to the Abrahamic Great Flood, and the terminus point for the same great cycle.[203] This is a good example of the cultural transmission of ideas between Palestine, Persia, and India.

---

[199] Ibid., 39, lines 11 and 13.

[200] K. Yamamoto and Charles Burnett, *Abū Ma'shar on Historical Astrology: The Book of Religions and Dynasties on Great Conjunctions*, Two Volumes (Leiden: Brill, 2000), xiv.

[201] Pingree, *BTB*, 44.

[202] Ibid.

[203] Ibid.

1.10. *SFAR MALWAŠIA*: DESCRIPTION AND DATING

The Mandaic language is found on three principle mediums: paper scrolls called **diuan**, lead and copper amulets containing spells, and incantation bowls.[204] Lady Drower wrote in 1937, "The majority of the manuscripts I have handled in Iraq are not old, although I possess a sixteenth century copy of the *Tafsir Paghra* (D.C. 60). I am told that no Mandaean manuscript older that the sixteenth century exists in European libraries, indeed no European library has even a representative collection."[205] According to Yamauchi, the earliest extant manuscripts date from the eighth century CE, the incantation or magic bowls are pre–Islamic, and the amulets featuring the earliest Mandaic writing date to 400 CE.[206] The content of some Mandaean literature is datable to the first and second centuries CE.[207] The *Sfar MalwaŠia* is not a **diuan**, or scroll, but a **kurasa**, an unbound manuscript made of loose sheets.[208] Lupieri dates the *Sfar MalwaŠia* to the sixth to sixteenth centuries.[209] These dates appear to have been origi-

---

[204] Edwin M. Yamauchi, "Aramaic Magic Bowls," *Journal of the American Oriental Society* 85, no. 4 (October 1, 1965): 511–523; McCullough, *Jewish and Mandaean Incantation Bowls in the Royal Ontario Museum.*

[205] Drower, *MII*, 22.

[206] Yamauchi, *MIT*; Montgomery, *Aramaic Incantation Texts from Nippur.*

[207] Lupieri, *TLG*, 163; Müller-Kessler, "The Mandaeans and the Question of Their Origin," 53.

[208] Drower, *SM*, 1.

[209] Lupieri, *TLG*, 58.

nally proposed by the German Mandaean and Gnostic researcher Kurt Rudolph in 1976.[210]

Lady Drower published her translation of the *Sfar Malwašia* in 1949. The translation is based on three manuscripts dated 1247 AH, 1212 AH, and 1350 AH, the equivalent to 1832, 1798, and 1932 of our Common Era. The English translation is 193 pages long. The book also includes tables for the Mandaic letters and numbers and indexes of noteworthy phrases and place names. A facsimile of the Mandaic text, presumably her own copy, is 289 pages long and paginated apparently by Drower. (The numbers are Arabic, not Mandaic.) According to Drower, the *Sfar Malwašia* is a collection of writings from many sources and contains two distinct parts.[211] The first part is properly called the *Sfar Malwašia*. The second part was cobbled onto the first, and Drower points out that the two parts have separate colophons listing different copyists and dates.

There are hints of manuscripts here and there, but few that I can confirm. For example, the pivotal Assyriologist Henry C. Rawlinson (British, 1810–1895) mentions the existence of Mandaean manuscripts in 1874, but I can find no further evidence of them.[212] There are only a handful of known copies of the *Sfar Malwašia*. Pallis cites Lidzbarski, who wrote that there are manuscripts in Berlin and Paris.[213] (Mark

---

[210] Buckley, *GSS*, 303. Kurt Rudolph, "Zum gegenwartigen Stand der mandaischen Religionsgeschichte," 146. It is unclear why these dates continue to be repeated in the academic literature. A possibility is that Rudolph is held in such esteem that even a date range of ten centuries is considered acceptable.

[211] Drower, *SM*, 2, 157, 158.

[212] Henry C. Rawlinson, "Royal Asiatic Society. Proceedings of the Fifty-First Anniversary Meeting of the Society, Held on the 18th of May, 1874," *Journal of the Royal Asiatic Society of Great Britain and Ireland* 7, no. 1, New Series (January 1, 1875): xx.

[213] Pallis, *Mandaean Studies*, 20.

Lidzbarski, Polish–German 1868–1928, was an important Semitist and translator. He worked with Drower on *A Mandaic Dictionary*.)

Buckley reports a privately owned copy of the *Sfar Malwaša* in the United States.[214] Gündüz says there are only three manuscripts, the same ones that Drower used for her translation.[215] Lupieri believes there were copies or portions of the *Sfar Malwaša* in Rome c. 1650 used by Abraham Ecchellensis (Lebanese, 1605–1664).[216] Nicholas Siouffi, a Kurd, worked on a manuscript in Paris c. 1880.[217] As far as I've been able to ascertain, the oldest extant copy of the *Sfar Malwaša* is dated 1798 CE—likely the same manuscript Siouffi studied and later used by Drower. It is currently held in the Bibliothèque Nationale in Paris.

Unrecognized copies of the *Sfar Malwaša* and other Mandaean texts may exist in rare book collections.[218] Mandaic texts occasionally are mislabeled as Syriac texts because Mandaic was considered a corrupt form of the Syriac language.[219] The more common texts are easier to identify simply because there is a greater chance of them being properly cataloged. For example, a copy of the *Ginzā* was collected in Syria by Robert Huntington (b. 1636–7) and given to the Bodleian

---

[214] Buckley, *GSS*, Mrs. Lamea Abbas Amara, 370.

[215] Gündüz, *The Knowledge of Life*, 59.

[216] Abraham Ecchellensis translated the Latin Bible into Arabic c. 1650 CE.

[217] Lupieri, *TLG*, 111, 119. Siouffi worked with the Theosophist G.R.S. Mead who wrote "*Gnostic John the Baptizer*."

[218] James F. McGrath, "Misidentified Mandaic Manuscript," Exploring Our Matrix, September 28, 2009, http://www.patheos.com/blogs/exploringourmatrix/2009/09/misidentified-mandaic-manuscript.html.

[219] Buckley, *GSS*, 97.

Library along with his entire collection of oriental manuscripts and coins, and was cataloged in a different collection.[220] Presumably there are books in private hands, perhaps scattered now across the globe with the diaspora of Mandaean refugees.

According to Gündüz, the references to Muslims in the Mandaean literature suggest that the arrival of Islam in the Persian Gulf provides a plausible motivation for consolidating the gnostic literature; he also notes that most extant manuscripts date from the eighteenth and nineteenth centuries.[221] Fortunately, all Mandaean manuscripts include colophons listing the name and dates of the copyists. Buckley has analyzed the colophons, not from the *Sfar Malwašia*, but from religious works, to construct a lineage of Mandaean scribes.[222] She dates the earliest historical scribe of Mandaean texts to 270 CE.

In the simplest terms, the *Sfar Malwašia* is an astrological reference book.[223] One reviewer of Drower's translation complained that none of the authors are Mandaean, "…hence the texts are of no help to students of Gnosticism. It is useful, however, to have access to ancient compilations reflecting the astrological beliefs of the various Jewish and Moslem [sic] communities inhabiting the land in which astronomy had its beginnings as a science… "[224] This is Drower's position as well: "(the authors)…are not Moslems [sic] or or-

---

[220] Ibid., 85. Buckley found copies of the *Ginzā* labed "Codex Nasaraeus" and "Liber Adami" which might be overlooked by a less thorough researcher .

[221] Gündüz, *The Knowledge of Life*, 55.

[222] Buckley, "The Colophons in the Canonical Prayerbook of the Mandaeans," 34.

[223] V.C.C. Collum, "Review: The Book of the Zodiac. by E. S. Drower," *Man* 51 (June 1, 1951): 85–86.

[224] Ibid·

thodox Jews as they worship alahia 'gods' nor is there anything to indicate that they are Mandaeans. They are 'god–fearing' and if the 'eye of the gods' is fixed on an individual, he or she enjoys good fortune."[225] The assessment is not entirely convincing. While it is true that there are few direct references to Mandaean mythology or cosmology, the book is not devoid of Mandaean religious identifiers. There is a lengthy section that describes how geography was assigned to the planets and zodiacal signs by Ptahil and Hibil Zawa.[226] Instructions on constructing amulets combine the native's astrological sign, or more likely the **malwaša** (star name) and religious invocations. Consider the instructions for a talisman constructed with astrology and a Mandaean prayer: "…born under Virgo, write 'I am clothed in garments of water.'"[227] Prayers and blessings are part of each section and colophon.

1.11. SUMMARY OF MANDAEAN STUDIES

This introduction attempts to establish some guidelines for a useful Mandaean narrative. The Mandaeans arose during the second or third centuries CE in the motley culture of Mesopotamia and the Persian Gulf. They are highly secretive, which some scholars have taken as a lack of clear theology. Secrecy and religious camouflage could also be part of the Mandaean response to living amongst hostile tribes. The Mandaeans are excellent craftsmen both with word and hand. As Gnostics, they are pessimistic; attempting to interpret their religion beyond that point is questionable. Jonas attributes the difficulty of isolating a gnostic doctrine to non–conformism,

---

[225] Drower, *SM*, 3.

[226] Ibid., 120–3.

[227] Ibid., 94.

contradictory metaphors, and an attitude of denial.[228] The British historian Tamsyn Barton writes, "It is often difficult to reconstruct the role of astrology in heretical sects. In the case of the Gnostics, since the finding of the Nag Hammadi library of Gnostic and Hermetic texts in Upper Egypt, it has been clearer that there is a close connection between Hermetism and Gnosticism."[229] Kurt Rudolph is more direct: "The external variety of Gnosis is naturally not accidental but evidently belongs to its very nature."[230] It is refreshing to encounter a viewpoint that chooses to accept rather than defend; it is not necessary to explain concepts that have proven to be both plastic and enduring.

Robert Zoller suggested "crypto–heathens" and "clandestine Sabians" to describe Muslim mystics in eleventh–century Spain.[231] Perhaps "Crypto–monotheists" might be an accurate term for the Mandaeans.

Over the centuries, the Mandaeans have demonstrated not only durability, but the ability to adapt in order to survive. This is expressed in their practice of astrology—an integrated part of their religion and part of their social identity. Lady Drower writes:

> The stars and the signs of the zodiac are the enemies of the soul. This we may, I think, look upon as refutation of the idea that man is the helpless victim of *heimarmene*, the play-

[228] Jonas, *The Gnostic Religion*, 42, 68, 267.

[229] Tamsyn Barton, *Ancient Astrology* (London: Routledge, 1994), 73.

[230] Kurt Rudolph, Gnosis: *The Nature and History of Gnosticism*, trans. P. W. Coxon, K. H. Kuhn, R. Wilson, vol. (German 2nd ed. 1980) (Edinburgh: T. & T. Clark, 1984), 53.

[231] Guido Bonatti, *Liber Astronomiae, Books I, II, III with Index*, trans. Robert Zoller and Rob Hand (Australia: Spica Publications, 1998), vii.

thing of the planets under the influence of which he was born. *Naṣiruta* is an urgent denial of fate, it is a call to the soul of man to hearken to its own *mana* which is at once an image and part of the Great *Mana*. If man listens to this call from within, he is proof against fate and the planets.[232]

---

[232] Drower, "Mandaean Polemic," 443.

2   ANAYLSIS OF MANDAEAN GENETHLIALOGICAL ASTROLOGY

2.1.   THE ASCENDANT

The astrological prognostications of the *Sfar Malwaśia* are exclusively based on the placement of the zodiac signs in the twelve mundane houses.[233] The American classical scholars Dorian Gieseler Greenbaum and Micah T. Ross write, "The ascendant marks the moment of birth within the circle of zodiacal signs, and orients the chart in time and space," and from the ascendant the topical areas of life are determined.[234] The topoi, or topics, are identified by zodiacal sign or by cal-

---

[233] The use of decans is discussed in section 2.3.

[234] Dorian Gieseler Greenbaum and Micah T. Ross, "The Role of Egypt in the Development of the Horoscope," in *Egypt in Transition* (Prague: Czech Institute of Egyptology, Faculty of Arts, Charles University in Prague, 2010), 160. 166.

culating out 30–degree segments from the ascendant.[235] The American scholar and astrologer Robert Hand has eloquently described the practice of using zodiacal signs as mundane houses.[236] The Mandaeans provide more evidence.

The distinction between zodiacal signs and mundane houses is a key development point in astrology. Epoch tables, ephemerides, and almanacs were all used to calculate horoscopes.[237] The calculation of planetary positions was not a common skill apart from the understanding of solar and lunar positions needed for maintaining religious calendars.[238] The addition of mundane houses and later the calculation of unequal houses required an understanding of spherical geometry that was the innovation of the Greeks.

The historian Otto Neugebauer (Austrian, 1899–1990) equates the first Egyptian calendars with star clocks based on the rising time of stars.[239] The classicist Daryn Lehoux describes how the phases of the stars were used in timekeeping, and acknowledges the awareness of the difference between 'real' and 'observed' stellar phases.[240] Evidence of the im-

---

[235] Kennedy and Pingree, *The Astrological History of Māshā'allāh*, 92.

[236] Robert Hand, "Signs as Houses (Places) in Ancient Astrology," in *The Winding Courses of the Stars: Essays in Ancient Astrology* (Bristol: Culture and Cosmos, 2008), 135–62.

[237] Alexander Jones, *Astronomical Papyri from Oxyrhynchus* (Philadelphia: American Philosophical Society, 1999), 35–47.

[238] David Juste, "Neither Observation nor Astronomical Tables: An Alternative Way of Computing the Planetary Longitudes in the Early Western Middle Ages," in *Studies in the History of the Exact Sciences in Honour of David Pingree* (Leiden: Brill, 2004), 182.

[239] O. Neugebauer, *The Exact Sciences in Antiquity*, 2nd ed. (New York: Dover, 1969), specifically the Egyptian decans, 81–4.

[240] Daryn Lehoux, *Astronomy, Weather, and Calendars in the Ancient World: Parapegmata and Related Texts in Classical and Near-Eastern Societies* (New York: Cambridge University Press, 2007), 10–11.

portance of the rising, culmination, and setting of stars is found very early in human culture; archeologists have discovered that some communities even made "false" horizons to normalize observations.[241] Neolithic monuments such as Stonehenge and Newgrange in the British Isles were erected at least in part to facilitate celestial timekeeping.[242] The Mandaean homeland is an environment where the horizon is not readily visible due to the topology and weather conditions.[243] The practice of observing phenomena on the horizon is unlikely.[244] Timekeeping in this type of environment utilizes gnomons and shadow clocks.[245] Pertinent to our discussion is that the Mandaeans used astrological techniques based on the rising zodiacal signs even though observing the rising constellations and planets was likely quite difficult, if not impossible.

By the time of the MUL.APIN (c. 1000 BCE), the rising and culmination of stars and planets are recorded by calendar

---

[241] Richard Bradley, *The Significance of Monuments: On the Shaping of Human Experience in Neolithic and Bronze Age Europe* (New York: Routledge, 1998), Chapter 8, "Theater in the round," on using monuments to define the horizon, or to create a "microcosm." 116–131.

[242] Campion, *Dawn of Astrology: A Cultural History of Western Astrology Volume One*, Chapter 2, "Prehistory: Myths and Megaliths" 15–34.

[243] The regional *Shamal* winds cause dust and sand storms that cause havoc throughout the Persian Gulf, on land and at sea. See, "Dust Storms, Sand Storms and Related NOAA Activities in the Middle East." *NOAA Magazine,* April 7, 2003. http://www.magazine.noaa.gov/stories/mag86.htm.

[244] Reeds are the principal material for structural construction. Mud construction is rare. Thesiger, *Marsh Arabs*, 75.

[245] Daniel Martin Varisco, *Medieval Agriculture and Islamic Science: The Almanac of a Yemeni Sultan* (Seattle: University of Washington Press, 1994), 81.

date.[246] By the fifth century BCE, a uniform reference grid of twelve equal sections of 30 degrees of longitude is used to measure locations on the great circle of the ecliptic, the path of the Sun across the sky.[247] The sections are named after constellations and are collectively known as the zodiac. The zodiac lost any connection or relevance to the actual constellations once it became a normalized system of plotting locations on the ecliptic.[248] The ecliptic, the celestial equator, and the horizon are called the great circles in astronomy.[249] The intersections of these great circles with the horizon and meridian mark the cardinal points of the astrological diagram

---

[246] Hermann Hunger and David Pingree, trans., *MUL.APIN: An Astronomical Compendium in Cuneiform*, Archiv Für Orientforschung (Horn: Berger, 1989), 137. More speculative is the discovery of star maps at the Paleolithic site of Lascaux in southwestern France which suggest that humans recorded the movement of stars as early as 17,000 years ago. "Lascaux Constellations," *Society for Interdisciplinary Studies*, October 3, 2010, http://www.sis-group.org.uk/news/lascaux-constellations.htm.

[247] Eleanor Robson, "Scholarly Conceptions and Quantifications of Time in Assyria and Babylonia, C.570-250 BCE," in *Time and Temporality in the Ancient World* (Philadelphia: University of Pennsylvania Museum of Archaeology and Anthropology, 2004), 77; Francesca Rochberg, *The Heavenly Writing: Divination, Horoscopy, and Astronomy in Mesopotamian Culture* (New York: Cambridge University Press, 2004), 128; Neugebauer, *The Exact Sciences in Antiquity*, 102.

[248] Rochberg, *The Heavenly Writing*, 128.

[249] F. Rochberg-Halton, "Elements of the Babylonian Contribution to Hellenistic Astrology," *Journal of the American Oriental Society* 108, no. 1 (January 1, 1988): 59.

and become known as the "favorable houses" or angular houses in Hellenistic astrology.[250]

Julius Firmicus Maternus (c. 280–360 CE) discusses the mundane houses, particularly the importance of the angular houses in Books V and VI of *Matheseos Libri*. He writes, "The first angles are the ascendant and the *Medium Caelum,* and the second the descendant and the *Imum Caelum.* From those four angles with their various significance the whole essence of the forecast is known."[251] According to the historian John D. North (British, 1934–2008), it was the emphasis on the cardines, or angles, which led to the development of further division of the astrological figure by latitude in addition to ecliptical longitude.[252] The major shift of Hellenistic astrology was to move the interpretation of stellar significations from sky observations and basic tables to abstract astrological nativities based on geometry.[253] The precise nature and meaning of these observations and the transition to calculations was described by the American Assyriologist Francesca Rochberg–Halton in 1991.[254]

There is a conceptual jump from timekeeping based on rising and culminating stars to the concept of the ecliptic divided into segments to represent specific areas of life.[255] With

---

[250] Firmicus Maternus, *Matheseos Libri VIII*, trans. Jean Rhys Bram, Reprint. (Abingdon, MD: Astrology Classics, 1975), (Book II 16) 47.

[251] Ibid., (Book VI 1.ii) 182.

[252] J. D. North, *Horoscopes and History* (London: The Warburg Institute, 1986), 6.

[253] Neugebauer, *The Exact Sciences in Antiquity*, 170.

[254] F. Rochberg-Halton, "Between Observation and Theory in Babylonian Astronomical Texts," *Journal of Near Eastern Studies* 50, no. 2 (April 1, 1991): 107–120.

[255] Campion, *Dawn of Astrology: A Cultural History of Western Astrology Volume One*, 203–4, 338 fn9.

few exceptions, all physical observations of celestial objects occur at night.[256] Daytime charts are mathematically calculated from tables, not based on physical observation of the planets and constellations[257] (although time and latitude can be found with shadow clocks and astrolabes). The introduction of the aphetic point and geometry effectively disconnected the astrological chart from the visible heavens and led to the development of hundreds of new techniques, including sect, aspects, lots, progressions, etc.[258] The Director of the Qumran Institute, Dr. Mladen Popović, writes, "The main difference between Babylonian and Greek horoscopy is that the former was not at all concerned with determining the ascendant at the time of birth, whereas this is the latter's primary concern."[259]

Al–Bīrūnī reminds the student that the houses are not equal in size because of the unequal hours of the day throughout the year: "That portion of the zodiac which arises on the eastern horizon at any particular time is called the sign of the ascendant…starting from the degree of the ascendant the zodiac belt be divided into twelve unequal parts, the first of these is known as the first 'house."[260] And Manilius, in Book III.6, chides any astrologer who used the short method of setting up the horoscope:

---

[256] Some celestial objects are visible in the diurnal sky: Venus and Jupiter are visible at periapsis during the day, comets and meteors are occasionally visible, and of course the Moon is visible for most of its cycle as long as it is above the horizon.

[257] Rochberg, *The Heavenly Writing*, 101–2.

[258] Holden, *A History of Horoscopic Astrology*, 13–4.

[259] Mladen Popović, *Reading the Human Body* (Leiden: Brill, 2007), 170.

[260] al-Bīrūnī, *BOI*, §245–256.

I know the Method, the Chaldaean Schools
Prescribe, but who can safely trust their
Rules?
To each ascending Sign, to find their Powers,
They equal time allow, that time two Hours:
But then from that Degree, from which the
Sun
Begins to start, his Daily Course to run...
But false the Rule: Oblique the Zodiak lies,
And Signs as near, or far remov'd in Skies,
Obliquely mount, or else directly rise.[261]

It is interesting that even Manilius is aware that some of
the technique has fallen out of astrological practice by his
time, the first century CE. He is reporting that some astrologers are not apparently aware of the obliquity of the ecliptic
and that this affects the rising times by the seasonal length of
day and night.[262] An alternative explanation is that astrologers
have intentionally chosen to abbreviate the technique, trading
long–hand for short–hand.[263] This lapse would only be possible if the astrologer were not trained in timekeeping, but was
instead 'book–learned.' The Hebrew scholar Jonathan
Ben–Dov points out that Jewish astrology was not as technical as the Greek and Indian forms because of the lack of

---

[261] M. Manilius, *The Five Books of Manilius*, trans. Thomas Creech,
(London, 1697). (American Federation of Astrologers, 1953),
Book III.6; 100.

[262] Twelve equal hours of daylight and twelve equal hours of night
make up a full day, or a *nychthemeron*. The length of day and night
hours is variable throughout the year.

[263] To be fair, it is also quite possible that the astrologer knows quite
well the course of the ecliptic and knows the difference between
solstice and equinox days. Perhaps Manilius is gently chastising
those astrologers who are using an approximations rather than
exact calculations. It is hard to know.

astronomical observations: "This meant that, as the other disciplines improved their methods of mathematical astronomy, the Jewish discipline gradually became more schematic."[264] This interpretation connects the sophistication of interpretation to the complexity of technique. Another view is given by the German scholar Georg Luck: "Not everyone who believed in the influence of the stars could possibly have understood the whole system and cast horoscopes himself," and he goes on to suggest that the common simplification of astrology is a "parody of the royal tradition."[265]

The Greek *hōroskopos* was one name given to the first house, from which all the other houses were counted, but it is truly a "multivalent" term used in many applications.[266] The Greek term *apheta* has the connotation of circuits, as in "where the chariot race begins the laps of the track."[267] Ptolemy used the term *aphetic* to describe five places in the natal chart from which the length of life is calculated.[268] The Arabic terms *hyleg* and *alcochoden* are used in an aphetic manner, and other points that can be used as the apheta are the Lot of Fortune, the Moon, the Sun, and the Lord of the Geniture. The American translator and historian James H. Holden cites Dorotheus, Valens, and Manilius, who all used the Lot of Fortune to begin the count.[269]

---

[264] Jonathan Ben-Dov, *Head of All Years: Astronomy and Calendars at Qumran in Their Ancient Context* (Leiden: Brill, 2008), 181.

[265] Georg Luck, *Arcana Mundi* (Baltimore: Johns Hopkins University Press, 1986), 313.

[266] Greenbaum and Ross, "The Role of Egypt in the Development of the Horoscope," 167. And, "...the meaning of the term 'horoscope' can sometimes be difficult to ascertain." 165.

[267] OED (1971), entry: aphesis, apheta, aphetic, pg. 384.

[268] Ptolemy, *Tetrabiblos*, Book III.10, 275.

[269] Holden, *A History of Horoscopic Astrology*, 91; Robert Hand, *Whole Sign Houses The Oldest House System* (Reston, VA: Arhat, 2000), 3.

The technique of deriving the count of mundane houses from different locations is a common feature of horoscopy from the Hellenistic period well into the Renaissance, and is widely used in Indian astrology. In Vedic astrology, the term *lagna* is equivalent to "house one" and is often qualified by how the count is started, for example, *jamna lagna*, *Chandra lagna*, *navamsha lagna*, etc. In Tajik astrology, the profected ascendant is called the *muntha*, which is related to the Persian term *intiha*.[270] The Arabic terms have become quite scrambled and often self–referencing. For example, Burnett uses the term 'prorogator' as the definition of *hyleg* in his translation of the tenth–century Arabian astrologer al–Qabīsī.[271] In the absence of consistent terminology, it is best to clarify the application and technique in question and not rely on jargon. In terms of the Mandaean astrological writing, we do not know exactly which techniques were used. We have only the interpretations, not the rules for drawing the figure.

2.2. TOPICAL HOUSES IN MANDAEAN ASTROLOGY

The first book of the *Sfar Malwašia* begins with genethlialogic summaries for each of the twelve possible ascending signs. The interpretation is determined by the zodiacal sign which occupies the astrological first house, then follows the topical order of the mundane houses. In brief, it is a generic book of horoscopy by the ascendant, not dissimilar to some modern sun–sign analysis books. The significance of this is that the text is not truly technical; a non–astrologer can read and understand it. (However, in Mandaean culture only the priests can read Mandaic, so the work is not what we

---

[270] Pingree, *BTB*, 90.

[271] Charles Burnett, Keiji Yamamoto, and Michio Yano, *Al-Qabīsī (Alcabitius): The Introduction to Astrology* (London: The Warburg Institute, 2004).

would consider a popular work for the general reader.) A complete topical prognostication is provided for each rising sign. (See sample horoscopes in Appendix B.)

According to Rochberg, "The zodiac of twelve signs of equal 30–degree length had its origin in Babylonia sometime during the fifth century B.C., the period of the development of scientific mathematical astronomy, and was invented for use in astronomical computation, not divination."[272] The next question is, what topics of life are covered by which houses in various astrological systems?

Mandaean house topics appear to be generally compatible with all the lists of house topics. Both Mandaic and Greek do not use topical names for the first and tenth houses but use the astronomical terms, an indication of the importance of these angular houses. The Mandaeans keep the seventh house gender neutral by recognizing the significance of the relationship rather than the gender–specific participant. The ninth house has a poignant meaning for Mandaeans: As gnostics, they live in exile from their god, far from their heavenly home. Otherwise, the topical areas of each mundane house are basically consistent.

The linguist D. N. MacKenzie (British, 1926–2001) provides the Pahlavi astrological house names, commenting, "As the number of houses, so the attributes of each house, i.e. the aspects of human life which they were supposed to affect, proliferated in the course of time. This accounts for the fact

---

[272] F. Rochberg-Halton, "New Evidence for the History of Astrology," *Journal of Near Eastern Studies* 43, no. 2 (April 1, 1984): 121.

Mandaic	Greek	Sanskrit	Arabic
Ascendant	I, Horoscope, ὡροσκόπος	1 (Lagna) Body, *Tanu*	1 (Ascendant) Body, Life, Conditions
Money-bag: **kisa**	II, Gate of Hades, Ἅιδου πύλη	2 Wealth, *Dhana*	2 Wealth, Livelihood
Brethren/his brother: **ahla**	III, Goddess, Θεά (*i.e.* moon)	3 Brothers, *Sahaja*	3 Brothers, Sisters, Law, Religion
Parents: **abahata**	IV, Lower midheaven, ὑπογεῖον;	4 Happiness, *Sukha*	4 Father, Fixed Property
Children: **bnia**	V, Good Fortune, ἀγαθὴ τύχη	5 Children, *Putra*	5 Children, Messengers
Pains and Blemishes: **kirla umumia**	VI, Bad Fortune, κακὴ τύχη	6 Enemies, *Ripu*	6 Illness, Slaves
Nuptial Rejoicings: **hilula**	VII, Occident, δύσις	7 Wife, *Kalatra*	7 Women, Marriage, Oppositions
Death/His Death: **muta**	VIII, Beginning of Death, ἀρχὴ θανάτου	8 Death, *Mrtyu*	8 Fear, Death, Inheritance
Absence from Home/Exile: **bit kalluta**	IX, God, Θεός (*i.e.* sun)	9 Cosmic Law, *Dharma*	9 Journey, Religion, Philosophy
Culmination/ "midst of the heavens": **mișat ešumia**	X, Midheaven, μεσουράνημα	10 Deeds, *Karma*	10 Authority, the King, Mothers
Good Fortune: **gada ṭaba**	XI, Good Daemon, ἀγαθὸς δαίμων	11 Gains, *Labha*	11 Hope, Good Fortune
Poor Fortune: **gada šapla**	XII, Bad Daemon, κακὸς δαίμων	12 Losses, *Vyaya*	12 Enemies, Misfortune, Grief

Table 2.1: Comparing Mandaic, Greek, Sanskrit, and Arabic topics for the twelve mundane houses that represent the activity areas, or topics, in an individual's life. [273]

---

[273] Drower, *SM*, I am grateful to Charles G. Häberl for translation assistance of Mandaic terms; O. Neugebauer and H. B. Van

that some of the [Pahlavi] names of the houses do not represent their 'basic' attributes."[274] The names used for the mundane houses are compared to see how astrological concepts are modified between oriental and occidental languages.

No.	Pahlavi	Translation	Latin
I	Gyānān	souls	Vita–Life
II	Kīsagān	purses	Lucrum–Wealth
III	brādarān	brothers	Fratres–Brethren
IV	pedištān	abodes ?	Parentes–Parents
V	frazandān	offspring	Filii–Children
VI	waštagān	the sick	Valetudo–Health
VII	wayōdagān	nuptials	Nuptiae–Marriage
VIII	margān	deaths	Mors–Death
IX	kārdāgān	travellers	Peregrinatio–Travels
X	mayān ī asmān	(medium caelum)	Honores, Actus–Honours, Deeds
XI	farroxān	the fortunate	Amici, Beneficia–Friends, Good Deeds
XII	dušfarragān	the unfortunate	Inimici, Carcer–Enemies, Prison

Table 2.2 The Palahvi and Latin house names according to MacKenzie.[275]

Hoesen, *Greek Horoscopes* (Philadelphia: American Philosophical Society, 1987), 8; Alexandrinus Paulus, *Late Classical Astrology: Paulus Alexandrinus and Olympiodorus*, ed. Rob Hand, trans. Dorian Gieseler Greenbaum (Reston, VA: Arhat, 2001), 111–118; David Pingree, *The Yavanajataka of Sphujidhvaja* (Cambridge, MA: Harvard University Press, 1978), 218; David Pingree, *Vrddhayavanajataka of Minaraja: Vol. II* (Baroda: Oriental Institute, 1976), I am grateful to Ronnie Gale Dryer for translation assistance of Sanskrit terms; Abū Maʿshar, *The Abbreviation of the Introduction to Astrology (Arhat)*, trans. Charles Burnett (Reston, VA: Arhat, 1997), 11–2.

[274] D. N. MacKenzie, "Zoroastrian Astrology in the 'Bundahišn'," *Bulletin of the School of Oriental and African Studies, University of London* 27, no. 3 (January 1, 1964): 526.

[275] Ibid.

In the *Sfar Malwaśia,* the technique is to overlay the house system over the zodiac and make an interpretation. In both the Hellenistic and Sanskrit systems, the evaluation of mundane topics is far more elaborate. The Hellenistic and Arabic astrologers universally consider the condition of the house ruler as critical to assessing the condition of topics assigned to the houses. This is a technique completely absent from the Mandaean astrological literature.

Sample horoscopes are found in Appendix B. Here are some general observations of house prognostications from the *Sfar Malwaśia* for a man's horoscope with a Scorpio ascendant.[276] The second house of 'wealth' provides a description of the native's working life, or how the native will earn wealth. The fifth house does not predict great progeny for the native, which is odd, because Pisces, the fifth house in our sample horoscope, is considered a fertile sign.[277] In comparison, the *Yavanajataka* says that a Scorpio ascendant will result in "a wealth of sons."[278] And in another portion of the *Sfar Malwaśia,* it is written that a man whose ascendant sign is Scorpio will have twelve children.[279] Some of the topical predictions do not align perfectly with the house topics. For example, the eighth house of 'death' provides information on illness, but not the means of death, unless the reference to an iron tool is a reference to Saturn and old age.[280] The ninth house has a secondary message if considered in the light of Mandaean religion: "He will be blind of understanding..." describes the natural condition of a novice gnostic.

---

[276] Drower, *SM*, 24–7.

[277] al-Bīrūnī, *BOI*, §354. Fertile and Barren signs.

[278] Pingree, *Vrddhayavanajataka of Minaraja*, 56–7.

[279] Drower, *SM*, 93.

[280] Iron is associated with agricultural tools, and therefore connected with Saturn, the planet of old age.

"…Divulges to no one…" could be a reference to the secrecy
of Mandaean rituals. "He likes the society of others…" may
refer to the commerce between Mandaean craftspeople and
their non–Mandaean customers.

2.3.   DECANS AS AN ASTROLOGICAL ARTIFACT

The division of each sign into three 10–degree portions are
called *decans* or *faces*.[281] They are used in Hellenistic, Jyotisha,
and Arabic astrology, but are derived from the thirty–six
Egyptian decans. The Egyptians used the rising of thirty–six
stars as hour markers.[282] The decans are therefore a very ancient principle that actually predates the zodiac.[283] Greenbaum
and Ross write that there are three different systems of
decans, and find connections between the Egyptian and Babylonian material.[284] The American astrologer and translator
Benjamin Dykes suggests that the more ancient application
of *faces* points to the use of images and symbology, where
later applications were given planetary rulership to align with

[281] Abraham Ibn Ezra, *The Beginning of Wisdom*, ed. Rob Hand, trans.
Meira B. Epstein (Reston, VA: Arhat, 1998), i; Varāhamihira, *Brihat
Jataka*, trans. Prof. P.S. Sastri (Delhi: Ranjan Publications, 1995),
207–15; David Pingree, "Antiochus and Rhetorius," *Classical
Philology* 72, no. 3 (July 1, 1977): 207, Pingree suggests the term
"masks" from Antiochus (Porphyrius 47).

[282] Greenbaum and Ross, "The Role of Egypt in the Development
of the Horoscope," 155, 160.

[283] Neugebauer and Van Hoesen, *Greek Horoscopes*, 5; Barton, *Ancient
Astrology*, 20.

[284] Greenbaum and Ross, "The Role of Egypt in the Development
of the Horoscope," 150, citing Parker, 1959; Ross 2007.

Hellenistic astrology.[285] The symbolic decans are listed in the *Yavanajataka* chapter 2, and in the *Brihat Jataka* chapter 27.[286]

Writing in 1029 CE, al–Bīrūnī summarizes the faces and the decans, and their rulerships:

> §450: The so–called 'figures' are in reality also the faces, but so called because the Greeks, Hindus, and Babylonians associated with each face as it arose the figure of a personage human or divine, and in the case of the Greeks the faces were also associated with such of the other 48 constellations ascending at the same time...

> §451: By the Hindus these thirds of a sign are called darigan or Drikan (decanate) but their lords are different from those of the faces, because other first decanate has as lord other lord of the whole signs, the second, the lord of the fifth sign from it, and third, the lord of the ninths sign.[287]

The Mandaeans use the system based on the Chaldean planetary order and sometimes include the rising decan of the first house as part of the natal prognostications. For example, a Leo ascendant birth, "If at the beginning, ...will be under Saturn. He will be broad of chest, and contemptuous... If in the middle he will be under Jupiter. He will be fair–skinned

---

[285] al-Kindi, *The Forty Chapters of Al-Kindi*, trans. Benjamin Dykes (Minneapolis, MN: Cazimi Press, 2011), 44n42.

[286] David Pingree, "The Indian Iconography of the Decans and Horâs," *Journal of the Warburg and Courtauld Institutes* 26, no. 4 (1963)

[287] al-Bīrūnī, *BOI*, §450–451.

and comely... If at the end, he will be under Mars. He will be tall and slight and sinewy."[288] This implies the ability to calculate the ascendant degree, not just the ascending sign. It also echoes the original Egyptian use of the decans for time-keeping.

Ascendant	First Decan	Second Decan	Third Decan	Lilly's Decans
Aries				Mars/Sun/Venus
Taurus				Mercury/Moon/Saturn
Gemini	Jupiter	Mars	Sun	Jupiter/Mars/Sun
Cancer	Venus			Venus/Mercury/Moon
Leo	Saturn	Jupiter	Mars	Saturn/Jupiter/Mars
Virgo	Sun		Mercury	Sun/Venus/Mercury
Libra			Venus	Moon/Saturn/Jupiter
Scorpio	Mars	Sun	Venus	Mars/Sun/Venus
Sagittarius	Mercury	Moon	Saturn	Mercury/Moon Saturn
Capricorn	Jupiter	Mars	Sun	Jupiter/Mars/Sun
Aquarius	Venus		Moon	Venus/Mercury/Moon
Pisces	Saturn	Jupiter	Mars	Saturn/Jupiter Mars

Table 2.3: Mandaean natal decans as listed in the *Sfar Malwašia* 9–37, compared to those in Lilly's *Christian Astrology*.[289]

Another curiosity is that in one section of the *Sfar Malwašia,* the decans are described as the head, loins, and tail of a sign.[290] This is reminiscent of the use of the quadrants by Paulus Alexandrinus in the fourth century CE to represent the different ages of life.[291] However, the use of the third

---

[288] Drower, *SM*, 16.

[289] William Lilly, *Christian Astrology*, (London: 1647). (Issaquah, WA: JustUs & Associates, 1997), (Book I.18) 104.

[290] Ibid., 97.

[291] Paulus, *Late Classical Astrology*, Introductory Matters §7, 15.

division of a sign for weather prediction, as found in Paulus, may be closer.[292] European astrologers such as William Lilly (British, 1602–1681) used the decans in determining planetary dignity. The Mandaean use of decans suggests the influence of early Egyptian astronomy and the later Alexandrian tradition of decans representing the beginning/middle/end of a time period.

Ascendant	Head	Loins	Tail	Lilly's Decans
Aries	Mars	Sun	Venus	Mars/Sun/Venus
Taurus	Mercury	Moon	Saturn	Mercury/Moon/Saturn
Gemini	Jupiter	Mars	Sun	Jupiter/Mars/Sun
Cancer	Venus	Mercury	Moon	Venus/Mercury/Moon
Leo	Saturn	Jupiter	Mars	Saturn/Jupiter/Mars
Virgo	Sun	Venus	Mercury	Sun/Venus/Mercury
Libra	Moon	Saturn	Jupiter	Moon/Saturn/Jupiter
Scorpio	Mars	Sun	Venus	Mars/Sun/Venus
Sagittarius	Mercury	Moon	Saturn	Mercury/Moon Saturn
Capricorn	Jupiter	Mars	Sun	Jupiter/Mars/Sun
Aquarius	Venus	Mercury	Moon	Venus/Mercury/Moon
Pisces	Saturn	Jupiter	Mars	Saturn/Jupiter Mars

Table 2.4: The complete decan list called Head/Loins/Tail found in the *Sfar Malwašia*, 97.

Paulus also used the decans as a measure of dignity, as did Lilly.[293] Al–Qabīsī followed, describing the power of a planet in its own decan as like that of "a man in his profession."[294] The system of decans became the basis of a rich iconography wherever it was introduced. The astrologer Meira B. Epstein

---

[292] Ptolemy, *Tetrabiblos*, II.11, 201.

[293] Paulus, *Late Classical Astrology*, 9–12. Teucer of Babylon and Antiochus also use decans or faces, as part of dignity calculations.

[294] Burnett, Yamamoto, and Yano, *Al-Qabīṣī (Alcabitius): The Introduction to Astrology*, 33.

translates Ibn Ezra's decans from *The Beginning of Wisdom,* and shows that there are not only different faces and decans, but also that the divisions were used for physiology, the weather, and religious imagery.[295] In Jyotisha. the first decan of Gemini is described as "a woman fond of needle work and ornaments / she is beautiful and without children. Her hands are lifted up and has attained puberty."[296] William Ramesey, a seventeenth-century British astrologer, described the same decan: "Jupiter...complete in all things, as it is a *face* of writing, calling of accounts, of giving and receiving of Petitions and Writings of no profit or utility."[297] The planetary rulership and images of the decans are combined in the *Picatrix,* an Arabic magical book used in the European Renaissance: "The image of a beautiful woman, experienced in dressmaking, with two calf and two horse emerges in the first phase of Gemini. This phase is also for Jupiter and it is complete in nature. It indicates recording and accountability, giving and taking, knowledge itself and seeking knowledge."[298]

The Mandaeans have no similar iconography for the decans. What they do offer are prognostications for the planetary ruler of the rising decan:

> Mars, he will be an unruly man resentful, evil
> sinful, thieving, a cheat and a liar, one whose
> heart is compassionate to none. He neither
> turns from the course before him nor is

---

[295] Ibn Ezra, *The Beginning of Wisdom,* Chapter II. Description of the faces of Aries, 14–25.

[296] Varāhamihira, *Brihat Jataka,* Chapter 27, 209.

[297] William Ramesey, *Astrologie Restored (in Four Books)* (London: Printed for Robert White, 1653), Book 2, 74.

[298] Maslamah ibn Ahmad al-Hakim, *Picatrix: The Goal of the Wise,* ed. William Kiesel, trans. Hashem Atallah (Seattle: Ouroboros Press, 2002), 145.

shamed out of it. He likes laying traps and incendiarism, killing and the forging of arms of war. And when he talks he utters folly.

Sun, he will be a ruler, lord of the land and provinces, and is beloved by his people. He will be compassionate, a good man, beloved by his servants, offspring, progeny, and tradesmen, and is fond of fine raiment and perfume.

Venus, he will be owner of money and wealth; if not, he will be an effeminate man: his star and his nature are feminine and he is fond of drums, and singing and dancing. He will own plenty of raiment, robes, and sweet perfume.

Mercury, he will be learned and wise, fond of solitude, a master of calculations and surveying, and will become astrology to a prince. He will be a poet, skilled in fine crafts such as carpenters, smiths, builder, tailors, and those who weave; calligraphy and all that is delicate, such as the setting up and fabrication of fine woven stuffs and products. He is versed in decorative chiseling and all that is beautiful.

Moon, he will be hasty, easily–offended, a fool that talketh rubbish——and a scatter brain and a drunkard resemble one! He is fond of hunting and travelling and journeys and cannot settle or remain in one place; he no sooner enters a place than he leaves it——if thy give him a dwelling, he asks to leave the place. When he asks it, they should not give it to him. He dislikes his children and home and prefers strangers, and does not return favors. He wanders off to work which is far away, and they will not be with him.[299]

2.4. ASTROLOGICAL PHYSIOLOGY AND MELOTHESIA

The identification of zodiacal signs with parts of the physical body is a component of iatromathematics, or medical astrology. The melothesia or 'zodiac' man is an easily recognizable feature reproduced faithfully even in today's almanacs and agricultural calendars. There is a rather abstract notion that the head corresponds to Aries, the neck to Taurus, and so forth, down to the feet, which correspond to the last zodiac sign, Pisces. This is abstract, because just as we have difficulty knowing the beginning and end of a zodiacal sign, there is also the difficulty of knowing where the head ends and the neck begins. The problem is more apparent when considering the Hermetic and Indian melothesia, which wrap the body of the cosmic man, like the *ouroboros*, around the zodiac with the head meeting the feet.[300] This is an illustrative example of the literal quandary of where the zodiac starts and ends.[301]

---

[299] Drower, *SM*, 97–8.

[300] Pingree, *YJS*, 199.

[301] Ptolemy, *Tetrabiblos* 1.10 "For this reason, although there is no natural beginning of the zodiac, since it is circle, they assume that the sign which begins with the vernal equinox, that of Aries, is the starting point of them all, making the excessive moisture of the spring the first part of the zodiac as though it were a living creature."

Different traditions use different systems of melothesias.[302] Melothesia can become quite complex, as the divisions of signs—such as the decans introduced earlier—can produce harmonic charts used to "fine–tune" the body part under question. According to the modern Indian physician and astrologer, Dr. K.S. Charak, at least five divisional charts in Jyotisha are to be used in medical astrology, including the drekkana chart.[303] Greenbaum and Ross consider the diversity of melothesias, along with other doctrines, as evidence that it is impossible for a single person or group to have invented genethlialogical astrology.[304]

Nevertheless, for the practicing astrologer, the melothesia was a critical tool of the trade, not for divination or medical diagnosis, but as a sort of client identification and pre–admission evaluation. First, the physical description found in the astrological chart should be consistent with the appearance of the native. Second, if the birth time was questionable or unknown, the melothesia could be used to determine the ascendant.[305] Third, the astrologer is able to discern an un-

---

[302] Zaehner, *Zurvan*, 162, for the comparison of the melothesia of the Zurvanites and that described in the Bundahišn.

[303] Dr. K. S. Charak, *Essentials of Medical Astrology* (Delhi: Uma Publications, 1994), 20–22, 43–44.

[304] Greenbaum and Ross, "The Role of Egypt in the Development of the Horoscope," 149–50.

[305] Personal experience, Kerala, India (2009). A method used commonly in India is to construct a whole sign chart with the current planetary positions for the day. The lagna, or first house is determined by environmental observation. The astrologer may determine the ascendant by noting the part of the body that the querant touches, e.g, the client touched his left elbow indicating the prominence of Gemini in the chart. Elaborate examples are given in the *Prasna Marga*, a textbook on horary astrology from India, c. 1650.

voiced or hidden issue based on the zodiacal melothesia.[306]

For our purposes, astrological physiology is a valuable and tangible path of the transmission of ideas, because it is documented from ancient times into the present period.[307] Explicitly, by examining cross–cultural examples, an attempt can be made to disentangle the purely Hellenistic principles from the attributes contributed by other cultures.

Pingree dates the origin of the zodiacal melothesia[308] to third or second century BCE Egypt, as an extension of the idea of cosmic sympathy between the macrocosm and microcosm.[309] This origin date is well within the time period of Ptolemaic rule in Egypt (305–30 BCE), or the Hellenistic period. The concept is firmly established throughout the region by the first century CE when, according to Popović, the literature shows "…many similarities between physiognomic writings from different cultures and ages…physiognomic knowledge varies, due to different culture, political, philosophical, religious and social settings."[310] Principal concepts, including zodiacal physiognomy identified from head to foot and the use of decans, are introduced. The methodology and application is then modified to meet indigenous needs. For example, some Jewish astrologers used the astrological physi-

---

[306] *Yavanajataka*, 53.1-2, if the question is real or imaginary, and the ascendant determining if the results are in the past, present or future.

[307] Popović, *Reading the Human Body*, 2.

[308] There are several types of melothesia. Here we specifically discuss the distribution of parts of the body to zodiacal signs. Parts of the body are also assigned correspondence to planets, houses, degrees, etc.

[309] Pingree, *YJS*, (The history of the melothesia.) 199–202.

[310] Popović, *Reading the Human Body*, 2.

ology based on the conception chart to determine the balance of "light and dark" spiritual qualities of the individual.[311]

Popović's work on two particular Qumran manuscripts has revealed an impressive catalog of astrological physiology in use in Palestine during the first century CE.[312] Popović contends that the Qumran manuscripts are of historical importance because they document the "transmission of certain astrological concepts to first–century BCE Palestine but not without some non–Hellenistic adaptions."[313] In *4QZodiacal Physiognomy* the melothesia technique does not predict the appearance of the person, but the appearance determines or confirms the horoscope, and the individual's spiritual qualities.[314] In other words, the astrological techniques have shifted away from astrology proper, and back to an early form of divination—that of physical observation—but it is based on astrological principles.

We find a similar situation in India c. 240 CE. A plethora of physiognomic traits are given in the *Yavanajataka of Sphu-*

---

[311] Francis Schmidt, "Ancient Jewish Astrology: An Attempt to Interpret 4QCryptic (4Q186)," trans. Jeffrey M. Green (Jerusalem (École Pratique des Hautes Études, Paris): The Orion Center for the Study of the Dead Sea Scrolls and Associated Literature, 1996),
http://orion.mscc.huji.ac.il/symposiums/1st/papers/Schmidt96.html#fn1.

[312] Popović, *Reading the Human Body*, 1. Dead Sea Scrolls 4Q186 and 4Q561. The 4QZodiacal Physiognomy were initially published by J. M. Allegro in 1956 and 1964. The history of the discovery and translation is given in Popović, Introduction.

[313] Ibid., 130. Also, "If the ascendant interpretation is correct, this means that 4QZodiacal Physiognomy shows evidence of the Hellenistic concern with determining the ascendant." Ibid., 170.

[314] Ibid., 33; Schmidt, "Ancient Jewish Astrology: An Attempt to Interpret 4QCryptic (4Q186)."

jidhvaja, a Sanskrit work dated to the second century CE.[315] The standard melothesia is given, as are many more physiological rulerships based on the various varga (divisional) charts that are used in Jyotisha.[316]

The spiritual component of the "zodiac man" is a broad field worthy of its own study. For now, let us understand that the Mandaeans believed that the human body was a representation of the cosmos, or cosmic body, and therefore held to be sacred in its own right.[317] The Primordial Man of the Mandaeans has strong affinities with the Zurvan 'endless form' and the Greek and Hermetic *Anthropos* (Ἄνθρωπος).[318] The Vedic equivalent can be found in the story of the "cosmic man" or *Puruṣa*, who is sacrificed and the parts of his body made into the parts of the world and human society.[319] The melothesia of the Mandaeans is both a practical tool and an expression of their cosmology.

2.5. WOMEN'S HOROSCOPY

The *Sfar Malwaśia* contains separate prognostications for men and for women. The innovation of a separate section for women's horoscopy is worthy of mention. In the classical

---

[315] Pingree, *YJS*, Pingree believes the Sanskrit verse was based on a Greek text written in Alexandria, c. 120 BCE.

[316] Ibid., 70–94. Chapter 27, Introduction; Chapter 28, Solar and Lunar Horas; Chapter 29, Drekkanas; Chapter 30, Saptamsas; Chapter 31, Navamshas.

[317] E. S Drower, *The Secret Adam : A Study of Nasoraean Gnosis* (London: Oxford University Press, 1960), xvii.

[318] Ibid., 22; Carl H. Kraeling, *Anthropos and Son of Man: A Study in the Religious Syncretism of the Hellenistic Orient (1927)* (Eugene, OR: Wipf & Stock Publishers, 2008).

[319] See *Ṛg Veda* Hymn XC. "Puruṣa"; *Srimad Bhagavatam* SB 2.6 "Purusha-sukta Confirmed"

Hellenistic system of astrology there are no separate techniques for male or female, young or old, poor or wealthy.[320] Diodorus (80–20 BCE) comments on how the Chaldean astrologers will tell the fortunes of even men "in private station."[321] Once individual horoscopes appear, the service seems to be available to everyone with access to an astrologer and the financial means to secure the service.[322] The implication is that the astrologer accommodates catholic techniques to individual circumstances including gender, age, and social class. When the Mandaeans separate the women from the men, it signals the beginning of a new astrological technique: comparing horoscopes for the purpose of evaluating compatibility and relationships.

According to Pingree, it was the Indians who first made the distinction in the fourth century CE: "The main innovations made by Minaraja in the field of genethlialogy were the development of a special field of women's horoscopy (*strijataka*) in *adhyayas* LVIII–VXII and the theory of the rays."[323] The rationale for a separate women's interpretation is explained by Varāhamihira (505–587 CE) in the *Brihat Jataka*: "Some results which a woman cannot enjoy by or for herself, those must be attributed to her husband…Anything about

---

[320] Barton, *Ancient Astrology*, 175.

[321] Diodorus Siculus, *Library of History, Volume II, Books 2.35-4.58*, trans. C. H. Oldfather, Loeb. (Cambridge, MA: Harvard University Press, 1935), II.29–30; 349.

[322] Greenbaum and Ross, "The Role of Egypt in the Development of the Horoscope," 177. "Once recorded by Greek authors, the practice of casting a horoscope–by any definition–found a wide audience and entered the western tradition."

[323] Pingree, *BTB*, 36. The rays measure the distance of a planet from its exaltation point and are a component of calculating planetary strength.

her husband is to be derived from her seventh house."[324] (Pingree notes that Varahamira was a "Maga Brahmana," meaning that his tradition came from both Greek and Iranian sources.[325]) The marriage union should indicate and support the advancement of the couple, whether that is measured in wealth or wisdom, piety or power. Particular attention is paid to the seventh house, which represents the husband in a woman's nativity, and the eighth house, which represents her death vis-à-vis her husband's demise.[326] Female horoscopy is an important part of Jyotisha. For example, in 1679 the Library of the Maharaja of Bikaner commissioned a copy of Ramacandra's *Strijataka,* a work on the "nativities of females" that confirms the inclusion of female horoscopy from the fourth century CE through the Mughal period.[327]

In the *Sfar Malwaśia,* predictions for men are given for the "ruling sign" they are born under. The predictions for women are "according to the hour in which she was born."[328] It is interesting that the **malwaša**, or star-name given to a child, is from the matrilineal side and is based on the numerology of the mother's rising sign.[329]

---

[324] Varāhamihira, *Brihat Jataka*, 176, Chapter XXIV.

[325] Pingree, *BTB*, 38. Pingree mentions an unpublished paper by A. Panaino.

[326] See also Parashara *Hora Shastra* Vol II, Chapter 82.

[327] Pingree, *BTB*, 99, citing D. Pingree, Census of the Exact Sciences in Sanskrit, 5 vols. (Philadelphia: American Philosophical Society, 1970), A 5, 462b–463a. 91. The Bikaner collection was assembled by the gifted bibliophile Anūpasiṃha (fl.1669–1698) and is an important source for texts of medieval Indian science and culture.

[328] Drower, *SM*, 37.

[329] Ibid., 68–9.

Female horoscopy is concerned with appearance (first house), property and speech (second house), the conditions and survival of siblings and parents (third and fourth houses), her success and failure at bringing male sons to term (fifth house), pains of childbirth and whether pain will pass in old age (six house), number of husbands and fidelity (seventh house), manner of death (eighth house), servants and ability to do magic (ninth house), social status and recognition (tenth house), appearance and temperament (eleventh house), and the critical years for illness (twelfth house.)[330] A sample horoscope for a woman is found in Appendix B.

2.6. PLANETARY ORDER[331]

Astrological prognostications by the ruling planet are provided separately for men and women.[332] The non–standard planetary order is Sun, Venus, Mercury, Moon, Saturn, Jupiter, and Mars. There is no explanation for why the Mandaeans list the planets in this sequence; however, the sequence is repeated for men and women, which would suggest that the order is intentional. A scribal error is not impossible. The colophon for this portion is quite long. It gives a lineage of seventeen copies of the text, including one copied by a woman, "the loose–leaved book which he copied for himself from the loose–leaved book of Anhar, daughter of Rabbi Sam Bihram."[333] The reference to loose pages may indicate that the odd order of planets is simply an error in page order. A similar error is found in the *Treatise of Shem*, where the order of

---

[330] Ibid., 37–55.

[331] Greenbaum and Ross, "The Role of Egypt in the Development of the Horoscope," The reader is encouraged to read this article for a fuller discussion of the issue of planetary orders. 151–3.

[332] Drower, *SM*, 56–68.

[333] Ibid., 68.

the last two zodiacal signs are switched.[334] Another odd planetary sequence is found in 2Enoch 30, where the order of
planets is Saturn, Venus, Mars, Sun, Jupiter, Mercury, and the
Moon.[335] The earliest cuneiform lists begin with the benefic
planets representing the most powerful deities, Jupiter and
Venus, and end with the malefic planet Mars.[336] Neugebauer
has noted that in individual horoscopes, the planets are simply
listed in the order as they are found in the zodiacal signs.[337]

2.7.   PLANETARY STRENGTHS

As demonstrated in the *Sfar Malwaśia,* the primary interpretive
technique is based on the mundane houses and the corresponding zodiacal sign in the astrological figure. This is a
striking contrast to other systems of astrology practiced during the same period. The Hellenistic astrologers universally
consider the condition of the house ruler as critical to assessing the condition of topics assigned to the houses.[338]
Dorotheus of Sidon, for example, uses the triplicity rulership
to evaluate strength, and this became standard practice in Ar-

---

[334] James H. Charlesworth, ed., *The Old Testament Pseudepigrapha, Two
Volumes* (Peabody, MA: Hendrickson, 2010), Vol. I, 473. Shem 11
and 12.

[335] Ibid., I.149–50; Thorndike, *Hmes,* on the Books of Enoch, 346.

[336] Hunger and Pingree, *MUL.APIN,* 147; David Brown,
Mesopotamian Planetary Astronomy-Astrology (Groningen: Styx, 2000),
193, "The so–called Seleucid period order of the planets."

[337] Neugebauer, *The Exact Sciences in Antiquity,* 169.

[338] Holden, A History of Horoscopic Astrology, 33.

abic astrology.[339] The inherent power a planet has in a given zodiacal degree is called 'essential dignity.'[340] The great Italian astrologer Guido Bonatti (died c. 1300) provides a quick summary of the dignities or strengths of planets in *Liber Astronomiae*:

> Each of the planets has powers in the signs, Some of them are by nature; some by accident. Those by nature are: house, exaltation, triplicity, term and face. Those by accident are joy, namely the joys of the planets of when they are in strong houses or places; and when they are received, i.e., when one receives another, like the other fortitudes which are spoken of in their own time and place. [341]

Other types of strength are accessed by speed, direction, phase, and aspects from other planets. However, the *Sfar Malwasia* does not consider planetary strength at all, only the influence of the zodiacal sign on the concerns of the mundane house.

---

[339] Dorotheus and David Pingree, *Carmen Astrologicum*, Pingree's Preface trans. by Dorian Gieseler Greenbaum. (Abingdon, MD: Astrology Classics Publishers, 2005); Pingree, *BTB*, 67,. references Abu Ma'shar using Dorothean style strength evaluations in the ninth century; Holden, *A History of Horoscopic Astrology*, 33.

[340] Lilly, *Christian Astrology*, (Book I.18) 101–3.

[341] Bonatti, *Liber Astronomiae, Books I, II, III with Index*, Book 2. XXVI, 30.

2.8. SUMMARY

This section has described characteristics of Mandaean astrology as applied to individuals. The uses of mundane houses and decans demonstrate the knowledge of the ascendant, but do not compare with the elaborate techniques documented by writers such as Ptolemy and Valens. Women's horoscopy is perhaps most interesting for establishing a timeframe of cultural transmission from India: Distinct material on women's horoscopy is found in Jyotisha works dated to the sixth century CE. It seems doubtful that the Mandaeans initiated the use of female horoscopies; therefore an early terminus date of sixth–seventh centuries CE is possible.

What is absent in the *Sfar Malwašia*, and all of the genethlialogic interpretations, is any kind of strength evaluation by astrological dignity. Prognostications are provided like aphorisms, without any type of explanation. Only in the medical sections are explanations found, yet these are based on numerology as often as astrology. For example, "if a person sickens on the seventh day of the moon, one should fear for him."[342] The prediction can be explained because seven is an evil number for the Mandaeans, or it could refer to the critical days of illness as put forward by Hippocrates.[343]

The interpretations in the *Sfar Malwašia* are entirely based on mundane activities in the native's life. For example, a woman with Taurus ruling and Cancer in the third house of brethren is given this prediction: "She will have brothers and sisters, but loses the brother older than herself. She will pray to the gods that two or three brothers may be preserved in life, and it will be well."[344] For a man with Taurus ruling and

---

[342] Drower, *SM*, 75.

[343] J. Lee Lehman, *Traditional Medical Astrology* (Atglen, PA: Schiffer Publishing, Ltd., 2011), 229, citing Hippocrates "Aphorisms" IV.xxiv.

[344] Drower, *SM*, 39.

Cancer brethren, the prediction is: "There will be quarrels with his brothers and sisters. The children of his father and mother will misuse him, or he will misuse them. But if favorable, the brothers will be friends."[345] These brief interpretations demonstrate the use of zodiac signs for evaluating the outcomes of the topics indicated by the mundane house, with no reference to rulership or dignity.

In the next chapter, Mandaean astrology techniques used for the community are examined, and more cultural links are established.

---

[345] Ibid., 7.

3 ANALYSIS OF MANDAEAN MUNDANE ASTROLOGY

3.1 MUNDANE ASTROLOGY

In Book II of the *Tetrabiblos,* Ptolemy explains that astrology has both a universal and an individual aspect: "Prognostication by astronomical means is divided into two great and principal parts, and since the first and more universal is that which relates to whole races countries, and cities, which is called general, and the second and more specific is that which relates to individual men, which is called genethlialogical."[346] According to the British author Michael Baigent, "The first known astrology was, on an official level at least, exclusively mundane astrology—concerned only with the welfare of the

---

[346] Ptolemy, *Tetrabiblos*, II.1, 117–9.

king and the State."[347] However, as Campion points out, the concept of a State or nation is a modern one: "People in former times were far more likely to identify themselves as part of a geographical area, as tenants of a particular landlord or as adherents of a religious sect."[348] One reason why the mundane astrology of the *Sfar Malwašia* is considered ancient is because references to 'the great king'[349] are thought to be an indication of Sassanian influence.[350] The title *Shāhanshāh*, or King of Kings[351] is in use by the Arsacid dynasty, 247 BCE–224 CE.[352] This logic is confusing because the Mandaeans never had their own king, and did not acknowledge the divinity of any monarch they lived under.

The universal or mundane astrological techniques found in the *Sfar Malwašia* are now examined. The 'annual' chart for the year is explained and its cultural connections to other Near Eastern new year practices demonstrated, particularly in regards to creation/destruction stories. The Babylonian Akitu festival and Mandaeans' **Dehwa Rabba** festival will be compared. Next, astrological timing techniques are discussed, fo-

[347] Charles Harvey, Nicholas Campion, and Michael Baigent, *Mundane Astrology: An Introduction to the Astrology of Nations & Groups*, Revised. (London: Thorsons Publishers, 1992), 19.

[348] Ibid., 95.

[349] Drower, *SM*, 110.

[350] Lupieri, *TLG*, 44; Drower, *SM*; Pingree, *BTB*.

[351] "Māshā'allāh's Zoroastrian Historical Astrology," in *Horoscopes and Public Spheres* (Berlin: Walter de Gruyter, 2005), 99. Pingree connects the exaltation of the planets and lunar nodes during the epoch of the sun and the Persian title: "The King of Kings is associated with the tenth millennium and with the sun."

[352] Parvaneh Pourshariati, *Decline and Fall of the Sasanian Empire: The Sasanian-Parthian Confederacy and the Arab Conquest of Iran* (London: I. B. Tauris, 2008), 48.

cusing on the planetary periods of the year and how they are determined.

The techniques of mundane astrology are based on astronomical events such as the eclipses of the luminaries, planetary ingresses into zodiac signs, the apparent (visible) changes in planetary speed and direction, and specific configurations such as Sassanian grand conjunctions.[353] Māshā'allāh (740–815 CE) was a Persian–Jewish astrologer from Basra and possibly knew Mandaeans and Mandaean priest–astrologers during his life. He provides basic instructions for the astrologer: "…set up these three higher, heavy, planets. Know that Venus and Mercury do not have importance at the entrance of the Sun into the first minute of Aries."[354] Annual charts can be calculated for the start of the civic or religious year; however, Ptolemy instructed the astrologer to use the syzygies of the Sun and Moon, especially those that produce eclipses.[355] The astrological chart is calculated for the geographical location in consideration and is viable for that region for a limited period of time, typically a year or a season, or until the event repeats.

According to Pingree, much of the mundane astrology in the *Sfar Malwašia* comes from the Sassanian tradition.[356] As noted above, mundane astrology was traditionally the provenance of kings. The Sassanians used astrology to research the rise and fall of religions and kingdoms, so why were the Man-

---

[353] Harvey, Campion, and Baigent, *Mundane Astrology*, Part Three: The Techniques; Manik Chand Jain, *Mundane Astrology* (Delhi: Sagar Publications, 1992); David Pingree, *The Thousands of Abū Ma'shar* (London: The Warburg Institute, 1968).

[354] Abū Ma'shar, *Historical Astrology*, trans. Keiji Yamamoto and Charles Burnett, vol. 1, The Arabic Original, Islamic Philosophy, Theology, and Science (Leiden: Brill, 2000), Masa'allah I.6; 547.

[355] Ptolemy, *Tetrabiblos*, II.4, 161.

[356] David Pingree, "Astronomy and Astrology in India and Iran," *Isis* 54, no. 2 (June 1, 1963): 229–246.

daeans—a people with a pessimistic religion and no king—interested in mundane astrology? There is no evidence in the *Sfar Malwašia* that they were interested in eschatology; they were simply making yearly prognostications. According to Drower, individual Mandaeans had their charts read and magical charms made for the coming year.[357] The answer may simply be that mundane astrological techniques came along with the genethlialogical, or vice versa.

3.2 THE SASSANIANS AND TRANSMISSION

During the Akkadian and Babylonian period astrology was a subset of omenology, which was universally practiced. The great Assyriologist Jean Bottéro (French, 1914–2007) pointed out that for the Mesopotamians, "everything in the world was divinatory."[358] Astrology and other forms of divination were used by priests for the benefit of the king as the proxy representative of the people. To determine the fate of the people, one only had to consider the omens for their regent. Pingree says that up to the Archaemenid period (c. 550–330 BCE) the use of celestial omens was controlled by the temples for the exclusive use of the king as "the principle [sic] means for the gods to signal their intentions to the king."[359] The connection between palace and temple, people and king was implicit, as it had always been implicit that the human presence on earth was to be of service to the gods.[360] The Dutch scholar Marc

---

[357] E. S. Drower, "The Mandaean New Year Festival," *Man* 36 (November 1, 1936): 185–188.

[358] Jean Bottéro, *Mesopotamia: Writing, Reasoning, and the Gods* (Chicago, IL: University Of Chicago Press, 1995), 105.

[359] Pingree, *BTB*, 18.

[360] Stephanie Dalley, "The Influence of Mesopotamia Upon Israel and the Bible," in *The Legacy of Mesopotamia* (Oxford: Oxford

Linssen writes, "This service involved providing everything the gods needed to lead a comfortable existence, and was normalized in order to avoid any mistakes or negligence, which would have had disastrous consequences for the people and their cities."[361]

The separation of general and specific prognostication is a function of the growing sophistication of astrological theories and techniques that are recorded in the cuneiform and manuscripts. As early as the second millennium these texts began spreading east and west from Mesopotamia.[362] Linssen observes that even during the Babylonian period, documents were held by temples and in the private libraries of wealthy families as well as in the professional collections of individual scribes.[363] However, owning a "book" was still an exceptional occurrence. When the Persians conquered Mesopotamia in 538 BCE, these practical considerations of owning literature were challenged as power and authority were redistributed. Baigent explains that the Persians "…broke the dominance of the temple over the country, and in the process diluted the immense power previously held by the baru–priests. The importance of this change cannot be overemphasized. For the stars could now officially be studied without having to subscribe to any religious doctrine."[364] This in effect laid the groundwork for the genethlialogical astrology created under

---

University Press, 1998), 65. The purpose of Man to serve the gods is established in the *Atrahasis*, c. 1700 BCE.

[361] Marc J. H. Linssen, *The Cults of Uruk and Babylon: The Temple Ritual Texts As Evidence for Hellenistic Cult Practises* (Leiden: Brill, 2003), 12.

[362] J. C. Greenfield and M. Sokoloff, "Astrological and Related Omen Texts in Jewish Palestinian Aramaic," *Journal of Near Eastern Studies* 48, no. 3 (July 1, 1989): 201n.

[363] Linssen, *The Cults of Uruk and Babylon*, 5.

[364] Harvey, Campion, and Baigent, *Mundane Astrology*, 27.

Hellenistic influence in the first and second centuries BCE, and the historical astrology created under the Sassanians after the third century CE.[365]

The Sassanian period began during the early third century and lasted until the Muslim conquests of the mid–seventh century. The state religion was Zoroastrianism, and the official language of the Empire was Pahlavi, or middle Persian.[366] Many important texts, such as the *Carmen Astrologicum* by Dorotheus of Sidon, were preserved in Pahlavi editions.[367] However, as the American historian Lester Ness notes, "Aramaic, the chief language of Iron Age Syria, eventually replaced Akkadian as the vernacular of Mesopotamia. Even during the following Hellenistic period, the Aramaic language continued to unite Persian–controlled Mesopotamia and Roman Syria."[368] During the Sassanian period, literature was written down and translated in many different languages.[369]

At least some of the Mandaean literature was written down in the Mandaic language under Sassanian rule. Mandaeans consider their books holy, due in part to literacy being limited to the priests. Yamauchi says, "To the Mandaeans writing is a sacred art and the letters of the alphabet represent the powers of life and of light."[370] Their literature, once codified,

---

[365] Shlomo Sela, *Abraham Ibn Ezra Book of the World*, Vol. Two (Leiden: Brill, 2009), Introduction, 14–28.

[366] George Rawlinson, *The Seven Great Monarchies of the Ancient Eastern World: The Seventh Monarchy: History of the Sassanian or New Persian Empire*, 1884.

[367] Dorotheus and Pingree, *Carmen Astrologicum*, 1, Preface.

[368] Lester J. Ness, *Written In The Stars: Ancient Zodiac Mosaics* (Shangri La Publications Ltd, 1999), 108.

[369] Greenfield and Sokoloff, "Astrological and Related Omen Texts in Jewish Palestinian Aramaic," 201–2.

[370] Yamauchi, *MIT*, 44.

became a cultural artifact, a religious family heirloom passed on through the generations. It is possible that the integrity of the Mandaic texts was protected to some degree because the families who owned the books held them sacred, even if they found the works unintelligible.

3.3. CREATION AND DESTRUCTION STORIES

Stories of creation, dissolution, and re-creation can be found in the Akkadian myth of *Atrahasis*, the Babylonian *Enûma Eliš*, Hesiod's *Theogeny*, and the Hebrew story of Noah. These myths of recurrence and cycles are "an archaic worldwide construction."[371] The cultural variations of the story give insight into the cosmological viewpoint of the people who told them. In the Akkadian story, humans never die, and the world becomes overpopulated. The god Enlil tells the other gods, "The noise of mankind has become too much," so a catastrophe is arranged to curb the population.[372] In this version, the gods make an imperfect world and decide to start over with the addition of mortality and infertility.[373] When the Mesopotamians recite the *Enûma Eliš*, they retell the creation story to reconfirm the mandate between god, king, and peo-

---

[371] Thomas McEvilley, *The Shape of Ancient Thought: Comparative Studies in Greek and Indian Philosophies*, 1st ed. (Allworth Press, 2001), 88. For Greek and Indian cyclical theories, see chapter three, 67–92.

[372] Stephanie Dalley, *Myths from Mesopotamia: Creation, the Flood, Gilgamesh, and Others*, Revised. (Oxford University Press, 2009), 23; Dalley, "The Influence of Mesopotamia Upon Israel and the Bible," 65–6.

[373] Dalley, *Myths from Mesopotamia*, Atrahasis III, 34; Benjamin R. Foster, *From Distant Days: Myths, Tales, and Poetry of Ancient Mesopotamia* (Bethesda, MD: CDL Publishers, 1995), 76–7.

ple. It is a recommitment that everyone will behave and follow the rules.[374]

In 1916 the great mythologist Albert J. Carnoy (Belgium, 1878–1961) identified fundamental differences in the Akkadian and Sumerian creation myths: For the Sumerians the world had always existed but was modified by water, while for the Akkadians the world was a by–product of the conflict between light and darkness.[375] In his view, the duality of Iranian cosmology was influenced by Akkadian mythology, while the concept of purification by water in Semitic religions suggests a Sumerian source. However, another idea pervading all Akkadian mythology is that there cannot be any world, nor any life, unless there is law and order, which is part of man's role in the universe.[376] This is quite similar to the Sanskrit term *ṛta*, which Carnoy explains thus: "The same word… expresses both cosmic and moral order, and that conception is absolutely essential both in the Vedas and in Mazdeism."[377]

In the Hebrew and Greek versions, the apocalypse is brought on by the misbehavior or sinfulness of mankind. In the Indian versions, these apocalypses lose animosity and become part of the natural rhythm of the cosmos. The world regularly ends in the Puranic literature; the cycles are connect-

---

[374] Dalley, *Myths from Mesopotamia*, 232; Julye Bidmead, *The Akitu Festival: Religious Continuity and Royal Legitimation in Mesopotamia* (Piscataway, NJ: Gorgias Press, 2002); Jean Bottéro, *Religion in Ancient Mesopotamia* (University Of Chicago Press, 2004).

[375] Albert J. Carnoy, "Iranian Views of Origins in Connection with Similar Babylonian Beliefs," *Journal of the American Oriental Society* 36 (1916): 300.

[376] Stephanie Dalley, "The Sassanian Period and Early Islam, C. AD 224-651," in *The Legacy of Mesopotamia* (Oxford: Oxford University Press, 1998), 163.

[377] Sanskrit. *ṛta*, Iranian. *arta* or *aša*. Carnoy, "Iranian Views of Origins in Connection with Similar Babylonian Beliefs," 307.

ed with the avatars of Vishnu and the in–and–out breaths of Brahma.[378] This aspect was passed on to the Sassanians and incorporated into their cosmology, which was applied to their development of historical astrology based on the cycles of the Great Conjunctions.

As Carnoy pointed out, "Myths have an essentially migratory existence."[379] These myths are transported back and forth along the land and sea trade routes.[380] Regional cults are found to absorb the propagated eschatological motifs: a beginning and an end to the world as we know it, punishment is followed by redemption or a new contract for behavior, duality defines duplicity—everything in the world is either good or bad, or a little of both. The Mandaeans have also integrated many of these concepts into their literature.

The Mandaeans believe in four great ages of man that make up the linear—not cyclical—process of time.[381] The first age began with Adam and Eve and ended under the power of the sword. The second age began with Ram and his consort Rud, and was destroyed by the power of fire.[382] The progenitors of the third age were Surbai and Sarhabil, and their apocalypse came by the power of water. We live in the

---

[378] Wendy Doniger O'Flaherty, *Hindu Myths: A Sourcebook Translated from the Sanskrit* (Penguin Classics, 1975), 43, 175. Also the *Matasya Purana*; Wendy Doniger and Brian K. Smith, trans., *The Laws of Manu*, Reprint. (Penguin Books, 1991), Book I 51–68, 9–11.

[379] Carnoy, "Iranian Views of Origins in Connection with Similar Babylonian Beliefs," 300.

[380] E. J. Keall, "Parthian Nippur and Vologases' Southern Strategy: A Hypothesis," *Journal of the American Oriental Society* 95, no. 4 (December 1975): 620–632.

[381] Lupieri, *TLG*, 49; Pallis, *Mandaean Studies*, 59–69, 140.

[382] Ibid, 143. Popular belief in the Eastern and Islamic world is that Adam and Eve lived in Ceylon. The Mandaeans put Ram and Rud, progenitors of the second age, in Ceylon.

fourth age, begun by Noah's son Shem and his wife Nuraita. This last world, our world, is destined to end by the power of air. Each age decreases in length, similar to the yuga system of the Hindus, and the sum of the four ages totals 480,000 years. The length of a complete cycle varies from culture to culture for example, the cycle according to Abū Ma'shar is 360,000 years.[383]

Another recurring motif is that of a primordial man, the Great Adam, who is also identified as the first person to die in every cosmic generation. In Zoroastrian mythology, Yima is both the first man and the first god to die.[384] His story is an allegory for the daily death/rebirth of the sun combined with the cyclical seasons. Jastrow makes the connection between the birth of Yima, the first man, and the Persian new year festival call Nauruz:

> Yima's Golden Age is the kingdom of spring, when everything is radiant and luxuriant and therefore the Nauruz–feast, the New Year's Day of the Persians occurring in March at the beginning of spring, is said to have been instituted by Yima. That season is destroyed by the demon of cold and frost, but the sun and life do not disappear forever from the world. They are kept in reserve for the next spring...[385]

[383] Pingree, *The Thousands of Abū Ma'shar*, 29, 27–37; E. S. Kennedy and B. L. van der Waerden, "The World-Year of the Persians," *Journal of the American Oriental Society* 83, no. 3 (1963): 320; al-Bīrūnī, *The Chronology of Ancient Nations*, 29. Sachau translates the revolutions of epochs and yugas as "star–cycles."

[384] Carnoy, "Iranian Views of Origins in Connection with Similar Babylonian Beliefs," 316, 318.

[385] Morris Jastrow, "Some Notes on 'The Monolith Inscription of Salmaneser II'," *Hebraica* 4, no. 4 (July 1, 1888): 313.

In Sanskrit the meaning of 'vara' is day; in Pahlavi, however, the meaning is that of safety, as in an enclosure or an ark. Therefore Yima is connected to the stories of Manu and Noah, tracing back to the Mesopotamian flood myths.[386] The Persians also take the 'Vara of Vima' as the mapping of a cosmic year to a cosmic day of the life of the primordial man.[387] Because the world has a creation, in effect, a birthday, the beginning of this world has a horoscope or astrological chart.[388] One of the most important functions of personal astrology was to predict survival and its antithesis, death. Historical astrology, under the Sassanians, becomes the study of the life and death of the worlds, the sub–periods are the life–times of empires and religions, and smaller–periods are the life–times of dynasties and countries.[389] The Sassanian scholars combined the mythologies of millennialism and astronomical cycles to categorize periods of history, and make predictions about future cycles.[390] As Pingree writes:

> Sassanian astrologers were famous as practitioners of the art of using the celestial science to reconstruct the political and religious history of the world through the theory of conjunctions, and to make general annual

---

[386] Mary Boyce, *Zoroastrians: Their Religious Beliefs and Practices* (London: Routledge & Kegan Paul Books, 1985), 95.

[387] Henry Corbin, *Spiritual Body and Celestial Earth* (Princeton, NJ: Princeton University Press, 1989), 24; Boyce, *Zoroastrians*, 12; Carnoy, "Iranian Views of Origins in Connection with Similar Babylonian Beliefs," 307.

[388] MacKenzie, "Zoroastrian Astrology in the 'Bundahišn'"; Pingree, "Astronomy and Astrology in India and Iran," 242. Similar themes are Thema Mundi, Mahapurusha, Gayomart, etc.

[389] Abū Maʿshar, *Historical Astrology*, 1:, The Arabic Original:11.

[390] Pingree, *The Thousands of Abū Maʿshar*, 57.

predictions on the basis of the horoscopes of the revolutions of the years and the prorogations of the *fardaris, intiha's* and *qismas.* Indeed, chapter 14 of the Mandaean *Book of the Zodiac,* which like much of that curious work, is based on a Sassanian original, contains annual predictions based on the progress of the *intiha'* through the twelve zodiacal signs.[391]

As stated previously, Ptolemy taught the use of the syzygies of the luminaries including eclipses, and planetary ingresses to zodiacal signs as the basic techniques of mundane astrology. Abū Ma'shar used the same format; however, he substitutes the conjunctions of the superior planets, Saturn, Jupiter and Mars.[392]

There are six elements found in Abū Ma'shar that represent Persian developments of Greek astrology:[393]

1) Persian astronomical tables and Indian time cycles (*yugas*)[394]
2) Conjunction theory
3) The *dawr* (a time–lord system)
4) The *fadar* (a time–lord system)
5) A particular use of mundane lots (calculated points)[395]
6) The doctrine of transits

---

[391] Pingree, *BTB*, 44.

[392] Abū Ma'shar, *Historical Astrology*, 1:, The Arabic Original:574.

[393] Ibid., 1:, The Arabic Original:581.

[394] Ibid., 1:, The Arabic Original:582.

[395] Paulus, *Late Classical Astrology*, On Lots.

The question for this study is, are any of these developments found in the Mandaean astrological literature? We do not know what planetary tables they were using, and this is not uncommon: Even Neugebauer lamented the lack of Byzantine or European medieval tables for research.[396] Without astronomical tables there can be no study of conjunctions or other planetary aspects. The *Sfar Malwašia* does not feature any 'lots' or other calculated points; however, it does include several time–lord systems.

3.4. THE AKITU AND OTHER ANNUAL FESTIVALS

The term *akitu* first appears in Sumerian texts of the third millennium BCE.[397] The name comes from the Akkadian loanword *akiti* for the cultic hut that is central to the cultic activities for the seasonal event.[398] Recall, one origin of the name "Mandaean" is from the name of their cultic hut called a **manda**. (The potential significance of this similarity is discussed below.)

The Semitic scholar Daniel E. Fleming includes the Akitu festival with a group of annual rituals conducted in Anatolian and Mesopotamian regions, involving parading the deity between the settlement and farming zones, "the removal of prominent deities from their urban situations to outside shrines, especially at the spring or fall axes (axis) of the annual cycle."[399] Current scholarly thought is that the festival consist-

---

[396] Neugebauer, *The Exact Sciences in Antiquity*, 55.

[397] Bidmead, *The Akitu Festival*; Mark E. Cohen, *The Cultic Calendars of the Ancient Near East* (Baltimore: CDL Publishers, 1993), 401–6; Daniel E. Fleming, *Time at Emar: The Cultic Calendar & the Rituals from the Diviner's House (Mesopotamian Civilizations 11)* (Winona Lake, IN: Eisenbrauns, 2000), 134.

[398] Fleming, *Time at Emar*, 134.

[399] Ibid., 138.

ed of a procession where the deity makes a triumphant and blessed entrance to the city. There is an ongoing discussion about whether the *akiti* shrine was the departure point or the destination for the processional.[400] The ceremony actually represents a cycle, like the seasons that make up the full cycle of a year. The important point is that the ceremony defines sacred space and mundane space on the terrestrial plane. (The Mandaeans have a similar practice as part of their festival.) The annual entrance of the deity, from beyond the city walls into the city proper, was a renewal of the contract between the god and the people: The god choose to live in the city and be served by the people; in return the people received protection and guidance from the deity.[401]

Baigent's summary of the Akitu festival is cogent but perhaps too simplistic: "In ancient Babylonia and Assyria the arrival of spring heralded the beginning of the year. The first month, *Nisannu*, began with the evening nearest to the spring equinox upon which the crescent Moon was still visible."[402] The quote illustrates a very real problem. It is possible to assume that he is referring to the first visibility of the crescent Moon after the New Moon, but he says "still visible," which suggests the days leading up to the New Moon. The Babylonian year is set by the solstices and equinoxes to mark the fifteenth day of the months numbered I, IV, VII and X.[403]

According to Mark E. Cohen's book *The Cultic Calendar of the Ancient Near East*, the new year was not always the beginning of an annual period of time, or even an annual event for some communities. He believes that in some districts the fes-

---

[400] Ibid.

[401] In modern terms, it was similar to renewing a service contract such as an insurance policy, or subscription service.

[402] Michael Baigent, *From the Omens of Babylon*, First ed. (London: Arkana, 1995), 140.

[403] Hunger and Pingree, *MUL.APIN*, 140.

tival was connected to seasons and set at the equinox points, which would explain the celebration at the first and seventh months of the solar year.[404] For example, the Zoroastrians used multiple calendars and practiced a double new year.[405] However, migrating Amorites from the western regions brought their own calendar systems, replacing the official calendars of Sumerian cities; the resulting ambiguity allowed older or just independent local calendars to also be used.[406] There the calendars were in flux by region, city, or tribe; for example, the new year was celebrated at the start of the first and seventh months at Ur, but at the full moon of the fourth and twelfth months at Nippur.[407]

Fleming's work on cultic calendars is specific to the cult practices at Emar, but also illustrates many regional differences.[408] Tablets found at Uruk and Nineveh list six different calendars that were in use concurrently.[409] In the Near East a 'new year' indicates any number of things, such as the start of a named year (King Darius says: The following is what I did in the third year of my rule…), the start of a fiscal or administrative year (the temple received during this year…), or the start of a religious or agricultural cycle. These institutional and indigenous (or, in Cohen's words, parochial and agricultural) calendars existed side by side.[410] A precise example of multiple calendars can be found in a Mandaic colophon, "the Haran Gawaita was set in order and completed on Friday the

---

[404] Cohen, *The Cultic Calendars of the Ancient Near East*, 401.

[405] Mary Boyce, "On the Calendar of Zoroastrian Feasts," *Bulletin of the School of Oriental and African Studies* 33, no. 3 (1970): 513–539.

[406] Cohen, *The Cultic Calendars of the Ancient Near East*, 248.

[407] Ibid., 401.

[408] Fleming, *Time at Emar*.

[409] Cohen, *The Cultic Calendars of the Ancient Near East*, 208, 240, 332.

[410] Ibid., 248.

twenty–sixth of the Month of Second Sowing, which is Nisan (in the sign of) the Ram, the year of Friday in the year one thousand and eighty–eight of Arab chronology…"[411]

Ben–Dov questions the modern understanding of calendars. He points out that the modern concept of calendars most often regards clerical, administration, civic, and religious procedures.[412] In Palestine, the Qumran calendars appear to have had yet another purpose: "The authors of the 'calendrical' texts were in fact far more interested in the harmony created by the conduct of the heavenly luminaries."[413] This is similar to the use of the Hindu *panchānga* or almanac, which is used to time religious sacrifices, and secular events such as marriage, to harmonious planetary positions.[414]

Hesiod commiserates with our blight in *Works and Days*, writing, "Everyone praises a different day but few know their natures. Sometimes a day is a stepmother, sometimes a mother."[415] To reiterate: Our concept of a year, usually defined as 365 solar days or the orbit of the earth around the sun, was not relevant to many Near Eastern communities. Particularly for agricultural communities, the two or three seasons that defined sowing, reaping, and resting periods were more important. Consider also, if the local calendar was based on local agriculture, then it would be subject to regional weather patterns. For example, in some areas of the Middle East sowing occurs in the fall and not the spring. However, even sow-

[411] E. S. Drower, *The Haran Gawaita and the Baptism of Hibil-Ziwa* (Rome: Biblioteca Apostolica Vaticana, 1953), (from the colophon) 22.

[412] Ben-Dov, *Head of All Years*, 3.

[413] Ibid.

[414] Lokamanya, *Vedic Chronology And Vedanga Jyotisha*, trans. Bal Gangadhar Tilak (Poona City, India: Messrs Tilak Bros., 1925), 39.

[415] Hesiod, *Works and Days*, trans. Hugh G. Evelyn-White, Loeb. (Cambridge, MA: Harvard University Press, 1914), ll. 822–828.

ing did not always indicate the beginning of a year. Preparation was more important for some communities, so the start of the year was initiated with the cleaning and sharpening of tools, dredging irrigation canals, and clearing fields.[416]

Nevertheless, by the middle of the second millennium, a common calendar establishing the month of Nisan/Nisannu as the first month of a solar year beginning in the spring was established.[417] Cohen writes, "This concept of a six–month equinox year appears to have been a major factor in the establishment of the cultic calendar throughout the Near East. In many locations there were parallel major festivals in the first and seventh month."[418]

3.5. THE DEHWA RABBA: THE MANDAEAN NEW YEAR

The Great New Year festival of the Mandaeans is called **Dehwa Rabba**.[419] An important part of the **Dehwa Rabba** ritual is obtaining astrological predictions from the priests for the coming year.[420] This festival has been compared to the ancient Babylonian Akitu festival.[421] However, the evidence demonstrates a mixture of Babylonian, Hellenistic, Tajik, and Arabic attributes.

---

[416] Cohen, *The Cultic Calendars of the Ancient Near East*, 91.

[417] Ibid., 12–13. Called the Standard Mesopotamian calendar.

[418] Ibid., 6–7.

[419] Alternate spelling is **Dihba Rba.**

[420] Drower, *MII*, 85; Buckley, *MAT*, 28–29.

[421] Drower, *MII*, 97fn; al-Bīrūnī, *The Chronology of Ancient Nations*, 201; Green, *The City of the Moon God*, 205.

The ceremonial activities of the **Dehwa Rabba** are documented by Lady Drower and Buckley.[422] Prior to sunset, all individuals practice the simple form of baptism that does not require a priest—three immersions in running water accompanied by prayers—then retire to their homes for a period of seclusion. They can eat only pre–prepared food and are not allowed to sleep for thirty–six hours beginning at sunset. Families will cloister together, although priests may build themselves separate ritual huts and sequester away from the general population.[423] The purpose of the seclusion is to avoid any kind of spiritual pollution that might occur with contact with the unclean world. The world is considered unclean at this time because the protective guardian spirits leave the earth to visit heaven. Touching an animal, swatting an insect, or drinking impure water is considered sinful and particularly dangerous during the **Dehwa Rabba**.[424]

A slightly different explanation is given by Buckley.[425] According to her source, the primary reason for seclusion is because the **Dehwa Rabba** festival commemorates the cosmic disaster that created the physical world. During those thirty–six hours the **natri** (watchers, spirits) abandon the material world and go up to the Light World. All living things are vulnerable during this time, and only food prepared in advance and stored within the house can be eaten. A separate isolation room is also prepared in the unfortunate case that someone dies during this time; the body is moved there until it is safe to perform the burial outside. The same room is available for

---

[422] Drower, *MII*, 85; Drower, "The Mandaean New Year Festival"; Buckley, *MAT*, 28–9.

[423] Compare to the *akiti* hut described in section 3.4

[424] Drower notes that non-Mandaean neighbors take care of animals during this period, a sign that the Mandaeans had good relations with some of their neighbors.

[425] Buckley, *MAT*, 28–9.

menstruating women, who are also considered unclean and dangerous.

In Gnosticism the creation of the physical world is a tragedy, and therefore the commemoration of the creation of the world is not a happy time. Rather than celebrating the spring, fecundity, and resurrection, the Mandaeans ceremonially remove themselves from the world. The storage of food within the house is evocative of the use of magic circles to demarcate sacred and pure spaces from those that are profane and dirty.[426] To this end, the Mandaeans use physical separation, or quarantine, for example, "…a line which encloses a person or object isolating pollution…and shutting out intrusion or pollution from without."[427]

After the sun rises on the second day, the Mandaeans ritually return to the world. Here, Drower relates the sequence of events:

> The first call is upon the high priest, from whom they learn the portents for the year, which they begin with ablutions and purification in the river on this second day. Individual as well as communal forecasts of good or bad fortune may be obtained from the priests, and if bad fortune is foreseen, a protective phylactery may be commissioned, since all priests are skilled in the art of writing amulets.[428]

Drower draws comparisons to the Akitu festival in which the Babylonian gods visit each other, and the god Nabu writes the tablets of destiny; she also compares the isolation of the

---

[426] Drower, *SM*, 127 fn3; Lupieri, *TLG*, 21, 31.

[427] Drower, *SM*, 127 fn3.

[428] Drower, "The Mandaean New Year Festival," 187.

Mandaeans to the myth of Tammuz's imprisonment and resurrection. The festival is a commemoration of the dead as well.[429] A ritual meal is produced and the eating of food is thought to nourish the ancestral spirits. Drower comments, "Not only does the ancient belief of the refreshment of the dead enter these meals, but that equally ancient belief which inspires our own sacraments, that the wheat which dies and rises again, and the water which changes dry dust into living green are only repetitions of the old mystery that death can be made the gate of life."[430]

3.6. COMPARING THE AKITU AND DEHWA RABBA

The philologist Martin Nilsson (Swedish, 1874–1967), in his 1920 book *Primitive Time–Reckoning*, makes the observation that the codification of a new year event that is celebrated uniformly by a group of people serves to legitimize their identity. He proposes that "the time reckoning of the years becomes also the history of the people" and "the adoption of the year–formulae of the main locality implies the complete subjugation of the town."[431] Nilsson's comment is well remembered when considering academic comparisons to the Babylonian Akitu festival and the Mandaean **Dehwa Rabba** festival. Finding commonality between the Akitu and the **Dehwa Rabba** is academic shorthand for saying that the

---

[429] Hämeen-Anttila, *The Last Pagans of Iraq*, Text 24, how the Sabians, Babylonians and Harranians mourn the death of Tammuz.

[430] Drower, "The Mandaean New Year Festival," 188; E. S. Drower, *Water into Wine* (John Murray Publishers Ltd, 1956).

[431] Martin P. Nilsson, *Primitive Time-reckoning; a Study in the Origins and First Development of the Art of Counting Time Among the Primitive and Early Culture Peoples*, trans. F. J. Fielden (Lund: Biblolife, 1920), 105.

Mandaeans are in some part Babylonian. In one sense this is correct, because both festivals occur in the geographical region known as Babylonia. The Mandaeans in this case become the descendants of the Chaldeans, otherwise known as Babylonians, living in the southern region.[432]

Heinrich Zimmern (1862–1931) was a German Assyriologist, not to be confused with Heinrich Robert Zimmer (1890–1943) who was a more accomplished German Indiologist. According to the archeologist Julye Bidmead, the first scholarly reference to the Akitu festival was Zimmern's 1906 writings, and these writings set the precedent to connect the Babylonian Akitu festival and other religious festivals including Hebrew, Christian, Roman, Persian, and even Arabic new year celebrations.[433] Bidmead does much to clarify the historiography of the festival, and her primary thesis connects the Akitu festival with establishing political and religious authority for the coming year, where "the earlier fertility aspects were superseded by political motives."[434] By the first millennium BCE the Akitu festival consists of a multiple–day celebration that includes the recitation of the creation myths. The king and the priesthood participate in the rituals, which can include the reenactment of the divine battles and marriages of the gods. Oracles are consulted and prophecies for the new year are made. By the common era, the festival is known as the "Akitu." The rituals now include a separate temple or cult hut outside of the city. A statue of the regional deity, such as Bel or Nabu, is paraded as part of cult activities.

The Mandaean festival meets many of these criteria both from the early and later periods. The **Dehwa Rabba** is a multiple–day affair. There is ritual purification, a ritual meal, and

---

[432] Hämeen-Anttila, *The Last Pagans of Iraq*, 40. His discussion of pagan and national identities is quite valuable.

[433] Bidmead, *The Akitu Festival*, 17.

[434] Ibid., 169.

the sacrifice of a dove. The stories of creation are read from the *Ginza*. Prophecies are made based on astrological calculations and the *Sfar Malwasia*. There is no ritual battle or marriage, but Drower connects the ritual meal with a marriage event. There is no royal procession because there is no social position equivalent to king or high priest, though there is a sort of parade prior to the ritual cloistering. These similarities could be very persuasive to argue lineage between the Akitu and the **Dehwa Rabba**. Caution is urged, though, because these elements are found in many new year festivals, practiced even into our own time by Jews (Yom Kippur), modern Assyrians (Kha b–Nisan), and Iranians (Noruz.)

The world view of the Mandaeans is gnostic, and the creation of the world is not a celebratory act, just as death is not a cause for grieving. In the Mandaean system, "true salvation comes with physical death, which allows the soul to rise. At the end of one's earthly existence, the search has come to an end; the time for questions is over, and the time for answers has finally arrived."[435] For the Mandaeans, telling the story of the creation was a grim reminder of their living sentence in an ill–formed world that was noisy, rude, and separate from the *Light Eternal*. The sixth–century Syrian mystic Stephen bar Sudaili took the same position, summarizing that this world is evil and will pass away. Arthur Frothingham (1859–1923), writing about Sudaili, categorized this belief as "pan–nihilistic."[436]

The element that is most compelling for this study is the practice of annual predictions for the community and the individual. The *Sfar Malwasia* is very clear: "These explanations were given to the *Nasuraiia* [Mandaeans], so that they might see, interpret, and know what will happen in the world

---

[435] Lupieri, *TLG*, 30.

[436] A. L. Frothingham, *Stephen Bar Sudaili the Syrian Mystic, and the Book of Hierotheos*. (Leyden [Leiden]: Brill, 1886), 49–50.

concerning high market prices, afflictions, murder, death, water, and rains and all worldly mishaps and misfortune."[437] The writer goes on to admonish the astrologer to "Look, look well and make no confusion lest thou be in fault before earthly rulers[438] and thy blunders deceive thee."[439] One is reminded of the Akkadian translator Simo Parpola's translation of a letter from an astrologer to the King: "Who? I repeat, he does not understand the difference between Mercury and Venus?"[440] However, the difference between the Assyrian astrologer and the Mandaean astrologer is significant: One is providing guidance and advice directly to the King, and the other is giving advice to a community and its individual members. There is no king or high priest who mediates between the astral powers and the earth in the Mandaean cosmology. It is the gift of knowledge that the astrologer provides, and the knowledge must be accurate. The actions taken based on that knowledge are up to the individual.

3.7. THE *SFAR MALWAŠIA*: PART I AND II

Mundane predictions are found in both Part I and Part II of the *Sfar Malwaša* which together form a **kusara**, or collection of loose pages. (Refer to section 1.8 for the contents.) In Drower's opinion, the first 255 manuscript pages made up the original text, and pages 257 through 288 of the manuscript were a separate document that was appended to the first por-

---

[437] Drower, *SM*, 125.

[438] "Earthly rulers" refers to the community leaders and not a king or monarch.

[439] Drower, *SM*, 125.

[440] Simo Parpola, *Letters from Assyrian and Babylonian Scholars*, vol. X (Helsinki University Press, 1993), 38.

tion.[441] She based this opinion on the colophons and appendices found in the different manuscript editions she worked with. She also notes that there are considerable spelling variations between the two sections.[442]

Part II is more fragmented and jumbled than the longer Part I. The first few paragraphs of Part II illustrate the disorganization: "If a cloud appears resembling a ram, the king of the Greeks will invest in Syria...If the first day of the year falls on a Sunday the winter will be temperate and the summer extremely hot."[443] It is not surprising that when scholars encountered such a hodge–podge of omen, calendar, economic and weather components, they labeled the *Sfar Malwašia* a corrupted text.

Translation pages	MSS pages	Summary
I:105–119	169–196	Greek calculation of new year, 19 Sabat (Jan/Feb)
I:120	196	Fragment—new or full moon?
I:120–125	196–206	Planetary and zodiacal significators for regions, countries, cities and people
II:159	257	Tammuz new year, by day of week (year begins in July)
II:160	258	Another calculation about the year
II:161	259	Arabic calculations "Muharram" (lunar new year)
II:193–194	285	Roman calculations "Kānūn al–Thānī" (year begins in January)

Table 3.1: Translation and facsimile pages of mundane astrology predictions in the *Sfar Malwašia*.

---

[441] Drower, *SM*, Translation of Part II, pp. 158–197.

[442] Ibid., 158.

[443] Ibid., 159.

The sections of Part II are shorter and contain redundancies with portions of Part I. For example, the exaltation signs of the planets are given on both pages 95 and 194. The mundane predictions for the new year that are found in both Part I and Part II and are listed in Table 3.1.

The most developed system occurs on pages 105–119 of the translation. It appears to use a European style calendar that begins the year in the winter, but the content of the prognostications are completely Near Eastern. The annual prognostications are based on the sign ruling the first day of the new year. This could refer either to the ascending sign for the actual day of the new year festival, or to the sign of the nearest new or full moon. We do not have the technical instructions to calculate the chart, only the prognostications which follow the protasis/apodosis format.[444] An example of a year's forecast:

> When the year comes to "brethren" of the world, it is set towards Gemini, Mercury governs it, and Jupiter and the sun are predominant. About the world this is said: that the year will be favorable; and there will be joy and sufficiency in the world and early (rising of the) waters (rivers), and in some places floods. There will be early rains and annual crops will flourish and be excellent. Barley and dates will be plentiful (though) blight will affect vintage grapes. The sons of Babylon will frequent banquets.[445]

There are many references to different geographical locations, including India and Egypt, but most predictions are

---

[444] Brown, *Mesopotamian Planetary Astronomy-Astrology*, 108.

[445] Drower, *SM*, 113.

about the environs of Mesopotamia. Warnings are given for extreme weather, disease, crop failure, and political riots. Although this section is the most detailed for yearly predictions, the segments progressively get briefer so that the predictions for the eighth through twelfth signs are quite short. There are occasional references to a planet located in a particular house, similar to the genethlialogical predictions previously examined. It appears to be a shorthand version of a more complicated system. Each section is identified by mundane house name, corresponding zodiacal sign, the planetary ruler and subrulers.

House No.	Mundane House Name	Zodiacal Sign	Planetary Ruler and Sub-rulers
1	"the life"	Aries	Mars
2	"moneybag"	Taurus	Venus, Dragon's Head
3	"brethren"	Gemini	Mercury, Jupiter Sun
4	"parents"	Cancer	Moon
5	"children"	Leo	Dragon's Head, Sun
6	"pains and blemishes"	Virgo	Mercury, Sun (Dragon's Tail?)
7	"nuptials"	Libra	Jupiter, Venus
8	"death"	Scorpio	Moon, Dragon's Tail
9	"absence from home"	Sagittarius	Jupiter
10	"medium caelum"	Capricorn	Mars
11	"good fortune"	Aquarius	Saturn, Jupiter
12	"Ill-fortune"	Pisces	Venus, Saturn

Table 3.2: Non-standard planetary governors, or dignity rulers in the *Sfar Malwašia*, 110-19.

The presence of the nodes of the moon—the Dragon's Head and the Dragon's Tail—suggest a date posterior to c. 500 CE and confirms an Indo–Iranian influence, as Pingree surmises: "The Sasanian concept would appear to be a reflection of the Indian."[446] The Persian chart of the world, the *Gayomart*, and the Indian chart of the *Mahapurusa* both assign the exaltation signs of the nodes to Gemini and Sagittarius.[447] The exaltation of the nodes confirms a connection between Pahlavi literature and the Mandaean astrological tradition.

3.8. ESSENE CALENDARS OF QUMRAN, JUBILEES, AND SHEM

Qumran Cave 4 is important for the large number of calendar texts found there: month and day lists, the schedule of holy seasons, both solar and lunar calendars, and mixed–types, including the *jubilee* method of timekeeping.[448] The calendar of jubilees uses a unit of time equivalent to the seven–day week. A seven–year period is called "a week of years," and seven weeks of years, or forty–nine years, is called a "jubilee."[449] It is a linear system of time. In comparison, section 3.3 on "Creation and Destruction Stories" uses cyclical correlations between a single day, a week of days, a year of days, etc. The association with dualism in cycles found first in the Zoroastrian cults in Persia are found in the Qumran materials as well: "This matter of cultic import finds mention in the description of the role played by the priests in the future War of the Sons of Light Against the Sons of Darkness."[450]

[446] Pingree, "Astronomy and Astrology in India and Iran," 242. Sasanian is an alternate spelling of Sassanian.

[447] Ibid.; "Māshā'allāh's Zoroastrian Historical Astrology," 99; North, *Horoscopes and History*, 167.

[448] Ben-Dov, *Head of All Years*; Shemaryahu Talmon, Jonathan Ben-Dov, and Uwe Glessmer, *Qumran Cave 4: XVI: Calendrical Texts* (Oxford: Oxford University Press, 2002), Ben–Dov's work is the principal source for the material in this section.

[449] Charlesworth, *OTP*, Vol. I, 39.

[450] Talmon, Ben-Dov, and Glessmer, *Qumran Cave 4*, 8. (1QM II 1–6).

The Mandaean material contains many techniques that use the day of the lunar month and the day of the week for prognostications. These are *kalandologions*, the predictions of the year based on the first day of the year, also found in Syriac and Hebrew texts.[451] The Semitic scholars J. C. Greenfield and M. Sokoloff write, "These types of texts go back into antiquity, and details may often be traced from Babylonian texts into the almanacs that have been popular from the Middle Ages into modern times."[452] This idea of contiguous cycles is elaborate in both Indian and Sassanian cosmologies; however, a perpetual calendar from Qumran is worth noting because of its emphasis on the Sun.

The significance of this calendar is that each new year and each season always begins on the same day of the week, in this case Wednesday. The second and third months of each season always start on the day of Friday and the day of Sunday. The community at Qumran used solar calendars, in part because of their interpretation of the creation story.[453] God made the sun and the moon and the stars on the fourth day of creation, as written in Genesis 1.14–19, Jubilees 2.8, and 2Enoch 30.2–6. The sun is given prominence, and so the solar year is promoted over the lunar calendar.[454] The Mandaean prognostications utilize all seven days of the week, and therefore is not compatible with this Qumran calendar.

451 Charlesworth, *OTP*, for example, see I.602, Introduction to the "Revelation of Ezra" and "The Treatise of Shem" .

452 Greenfield and Sokoloff, "Astrological and Related Omen Texts in Jewish Palestinian Aramaic," 212.

453 Eviatar Zerubavel, *The Seven Day Circle* (New York: Free Press, 1985), 71; Talmon, Ben-Dov, and Glessmer, *Qumran Cave 4*, 47.

454 Talmon, Ben-Dov, and Glessmer, *Qumran Cave 4*, 46–47.

Months	Days of the Week						
	Sunday	Monday	Tuesday	Wed.	Thursday	Friday	Sabbath
I, IV, VII, X				1	2	3	4
	5	6	7	8	9	10	11
	12	13	14	15	16	17	18
	19	20	21	22	23	24	25
	26	27	28	29	30		
II, V, VIII, XI						1	2
	3	4	5	6	7	8	9
	10	11	12	13	14	15	16
	17	18	19	20	21	22	23
	24	25	26	27	28	29	30
III, VI, IX, XII	1	2	3	4	5	6	7
	8	9	10	11	12	13	14
	15	16	17	18	19	20	21
	22	23	24	25	26	27	28
	29	30	31				

Table 3.3: Qumran perpetual calendar. 364 Day Solar Calendar, with identical annual quarters of thirteen weeks. Note that for each month, the first, fifteenth and twentyninth day will always fall on the same day of the week. (Based on Talmon, et. al.)[455]

Although the seven–day week is pervasive in the modern world and popular in the ancient world, it is not a "universal phenomenon." Eviatar Zerubavel, a writer on matters of time, believes there are three explanations for the adoption of a seven–day week: a complex divinatory system based on as-

[455] Ibid., 4.

tral science, a complex economy that requires regular market days, and the influence of "extra–natural liturgical cycles" as used in the Abrahamic religions.[456] The origin of the seven–day week he places squarely on the shoulders of the Greeks in second–century Alexandria, who successfully integrated the Egyptian practice of hourly division of the day and night, Babylonian planetary omens, and the Hellenistic order of the planets based on sidereal orbital periods.[457]

The Mandaeans record both the distance and speed of the planets. "These are the stars upon the days (of which?) calculation of the spheres must be made. The highest sphere, Saturn; the second, Jupiter; the third, Mars; the fourth, the sun; the fifth, Venus; the sixth, Mercury; the seventh, the moon." [458] The Mandaeans also recorded the length of time each planet takes to transit a zodiacal sign: "Saturn occupies (one zodiacal sign) thirty months; Jupiter, twelve months; Mars, forty–five days; the sun, thirty days; the moon, two and a half days; Venus, twenty–seven days; and Mercury occupies seventeen days."[459] These citations stand out in the material which, as noted, is more oriented toward interpretation, and less toward technical matters.

The *Book of Jubilees* provides another clue for the development of the week with its emphasis on the fourth day of creation, and the connection between sacred and mundane time, as the Canadian scholar James M. Scott writes:

> First, the antedating of the Festival of Weeks
> to the time of creation aptly illustrates the

[456] Zerubavel, *The Seven Day Circle*, 85.

[457] Ibid., 14. On planetary orders see..; Neugebauer, *The Exact Sciences in Antiquity*, 168–70; Pallis, *Mandaean Studies*, planetary lists in the *Ginzā*, 31–37.

[458] Drower, *SM*, 70–1.

[459] Ibid.

book's perspective on the origins of sacred time. For *Jubilees*, the creation of the sun on the fourth day set in motion an eternal rhythm that determines the immutable cycles of *all cultic practice in heaven and on earth*. Second, and closely related to this fact, there is a divinely intended correlation between cultic practice in heaven and on earth.[460]

The *Treatise of Shem* is of particular importance to the study of Mandaean astrology. This work is found in both Coptic and Arabic literature, and has a date of the late fifteenth century, although it could be as early as the first century BCE.[461] The manuscript is an astrological work but also represents the passage of knowledge from the time before Noah to the time after Noah. Shem is the transitional figure between antediluvian and postdiluvian biblical chronology[462]—the link to the last golden age, and the guide for the present dark age. It is not surprising that Shem is believed to be the progenitor of the Mandaeans.[463]

3.9. MUNDANE TIMING TECHNIQUES

There is a wide spectrum of timing calculations available in astrology: progressions, directions, solar arcs, Indian *dashas* and Arabic *fidarias*, Hellenistic *chronocrators*, etc[464]. The majority

---

[460] James M. Scott, *On Earth as in Heaven: The Restoration of Sacred Time and Sacred Space in the Book of Jubilees* (Leiden: Brill, 2005), 1.

[461] John C. Reeves, *Heralds of That Good Realm: Syro-Mesopotamian Gnosis and Jewish Traditions* (Leiden: Brill, 1996), 38.

[462] Ibid., 164. See Jub. 10:14, Jub. 19:14.

[463] Lupieri, *TLG*, 50, 51.

[464] Abraham Ibn Ezra, *The Beginning of Wisdom*, ed. Rob Hand, trans. Meira B. Epstein (Reston, VA: Arhat, 1998), For aspects and directions, see Chapter 10, 156–158; al-Bīrūnī, *BOI* 395: Firdaria

of these techniques follow a specific order of such as the planetary week–day lords or Indian Nakshatra lords. Some techniques set the order by planetary ascensional time or by degree of latitude. For annual mundane charts, the Mandaeans use a unique system of planetary periods not found in any other timing system.

The Mandaeans divide the year into planetary periods. The order follows the days of the week—Sun, Moon, Mars, Mercury, Jupiter, Venus, and Saturn—except that the planet Mars gets *two* periods, regardless of which day starts the new year. Each planet is allotted a forty–five day period, beginning with the lord of the year, except for Mars, which always gets two forty–five day periods. The double–Mars period is given for all seven of the possible yearly prognostications:

New Year starts on	Planetary cycle for the year is...
Sunday	Sun–Moon–MARS1–MARS2–Mercury–Jupiter–Venus–Saturn
Monday	Moon–MARS1–MARS2–Mercury–Jupiter–Venus–Saturn–Sun
Tuesday	MARS1–MARS2–Mercury–Jupiter–Venus–Saturn–Sun–Moon
Wednesday	Mercury–Jupiter–Venus–Saturn–Sun–Moon–MARS1–MARS2
Thursday	Jupiter–Venus–Saturn–Sun–Moon–MARS1–MARS2–Mercury
Friday	Venus–Saturn–Sun–Moon–MARS1–MARS2–Mercury–Jupiter
Saturday	Saturn–Sun–Moon–MARS1–MARS2–Mercury–Jupiter–Venus

Table 3.4: The unique double Mars planetary periods used by Mandaeans. See *Sfar Malwašia*, 105–10.

---

of Planets (Chronocrators), 239. Dashas, Parashara Horashatra Chapter 46.

It is uncommon for any timing system to call for a single planet to be given a double allotment.[465] The only system that produces a multiple occurrence of Mars is the order of the decans, where the first decan of Aries and the last decan of Pisces are both ruled by Mars, resulting in a double occurrence of Mars in the continuous sequence.[466] One also wonders why double the allotment of a malefic planet. The Mandaeans called Muslims "sons of the butcher" and assigned Mars as the planetary rulership of Islam.[467] Why not one of the benefic planets, or even the neutral Mercury? There is a plausible rational argument for Mercury, not Mars, getting double honor, because as lord of the fourth day of the week, Mercury symbolizes the fourth day of creation, when the luminaries came into being.

The length of planetary period is odd, but not impossible. Eight periods of forty–five days produces 360 days. Add five intercalculary days, and the result is a workable solar calendar, very similar to the Egyptian calendar. Forty–five days is also the midpoint of each of the seasons, as documented in very early periods.[468]

The *Sfar Malwašia* says that Mars takes forty–five days for the mean–time transit of a zodiac sign.[469] Is it possible that the Mandaeans gave Mars a double allotment because the

---

[465] Dorian Giesler Greenbaum has informed me that in Valens, *Anthology* IV. 4-10, Saturn receives two allotments in sequence because it rules both Capricorn and Aquarius.

[466] al-Kindi, *The Forty Chapters of Al-Kindi*, 43n39, Dykes makes the same observation.

[467] Drower, *The Haran Gawaita and the Baptism of Hibil-Ziwa*, 12.

[468] Ben-Dov, *Head of All Years*, 182. "The Mul.Apin and its related texts are based on the ideal year of 360 days, which comprises 12 month of 30 days each. The year is divided into four seasons of 90 days each."

[469] Drower, *SM*, 71.

planet stays in a sign for the same length of time as a quarter—season? Lupieri mentions that the Mandaeans believed the soul took forty—five days to cross the heavens after death and arrive at the throne of Abutar, the heavenly judge of souls.[470]

None of these proposals are very satisfying, and the matter remains a mystery.

3.10. TAJIK ASTROLOGY OF THE INDO–IRANIANS

Tajik or *tajika* astrology is Persian astrology written in Sanskrit. Pingree writes, "Tajika is an amalgam of elements from Indian and Arab/Persian genethlialogy,"[471] However, Pingree also claims that the original source of Tajik astrology is the *Yavanajataka*, a third century Sanskrit translation of an earlier Greek astrological text he dated to 149/150 CE.[472] To further complicate matters, the word *tajika* is the Sanskrit transliteration of the Pahlavi/Persian word for 'Arab.'[473] In the broadest application, Tajiks were non–Turkish Muslims, just like *Yavanas* were originally Greeks, but the term became used for any non–Arab people from the west.[474] Another term encountered is *Mleccha,* which is a social classification meaning the person is not a member of any traditional caste.[475] It is important to discern these terms in Sanskrit texts if the author is referring to a Greek, Persian, or Arab person; as the

---

[470] Lupieri, *TLG*, 31.

[471] Pingree, *BTB*, 87.

[472] Ibid., 79.

[473] Ibid., 79. Pahlavi "Tazig" and Persian "Tazi."

[474] Romila Thapar, *Early India: From the Origins to AD 1300* (Berkeley, CA: University of California Press, 2004), 160, 440.

[475] Ibid., 217, 440, 465.

historian Romila Thapar cautions, "The context of the term, therefore, is of the utmost importance in its specific uses."[476]

The *Tajikatantrasara* is not extant, but survives as quoted in Sanskrit anthologies. However the author, Samarasimha,[477] tells us that he lived in Saurastra—a port in Gujarat—and Pingree provisionally dates the work to 1274 CE.[478] The significance of the date is that Gujarat at this time was not under Muslim rule, but did have a large Muslim population of merchants.[479] Pingree sources Tajik astrology to the mixture of "commercial and intellectual interest" occurring on the Gujarat peninsula between Muslims, Hindus and Jains.[480]

The Mughal kingdom under Akbar took control of Gujarat in 1572, the same year we know that Nilankantha, an Indian from Dharmapura, served as *jyotisraja* or royal astrologer to Akbar.[481] In 1587 Nilankantha finished the *Tajikanilakanthi*, of which nearly 800 manuscript copies are known by Pingree.[482] In 1689 Anupasimha had a copy of Nilankanth's *Tajikanilakanthi* made for the Library of Maharaja of Bikaner.[483] We also have historical evidence of Mandaeans travelling between the Persian Gulf and the Malabar, both as traders and under the duress of Portuguese missionaries in the seventeenth century. What we cannot determine is if these traveling Mandaeans learned or transmitted astrological knowledge.

---

[476] Ibid., 440.

[477] Samarasimha=The Lion of Samara, my translation.

[478] Pingree, *BTB*, 81.

[479] Ibid.

[480] Ibid., 82.

[481] Ibid., 84.

[482] Ibid.

[483] Ibid., 102. See section 2.5 "Women's Horoscopy" above.

One characteristic found in Tajik astrology is the use of Arabic Parts, more properly called the Greek Lots. (Guido Bonatti, died c.1296–1300, first called these calculated points Arabic Parts in his *Liber Astronomiae*.[484]) The Greek Lots are a geometric construction based on the distance between two points on the ecliptic, added or subtracted from a third point.[485] Paulus in the fourth century describes more than one hundred lots.[486] Abū Maʿshar (787–886 CE) lists ninety–seven lots.[487]

What is interesting to our study is that Nilakantha's book lists fifty of these calculated points, called *sahams* in Sanskrit.[488] The Indian translator D.P. Saxena points out that it is uncommon and frankly unnecessary to calculate all fifty sahams. He gives the example of arranged marriages, where certain *sahams* would be helpful to determine an appropriate match for children aged 7–8, but not so useful for older children or adults.[489]

---

[484] Bonatti, *Liber Astronomiae, Books I, II, III with Index*; Robert Zoller, "Abū Maʿshar: Prince of Astrologers", revised 2000 1993, http://www.new-library.com/zoller/features/rz-article-abumashar.shtml.

[485] Dorian Gieseler Greenbaum, "Calculating the Lots of Fortune and Daemon in Hellenistic Astrology," in *The Winding Courses of the Stars : Essays in Ancient Astrology* (Bristol: Culture and Cosmos, 2008), The most recent scholarship on the Greek lots.

[486] Paulus, *Late Classical Astrology*, 41–44, 101–111. See Appendix I for a list of names and formulas for the Lots.

[487] al-Bīrūnī, *BOI*, §476; Robert Zoller, *The Arabic Parts in Astrology: A Lost Key to Prediction* (New York: Inner Traditions, 1989), 7.

[488] Neelkantha, *Tajik*, trans. D.P. Saxena (Delhi, India: Ranjan Publications, 2001), 89–116.

[489] Ibid., 115.

The Mandaeans do not have any technique comparable to the lots. Perhaps this is an example of a technique that was flourishing in parts of Persia and in India but did not make the transition into Mandaean astrology. Comparing the *Sfar Malwašia* with the Tajik, or Persian astrology, we can trace the importance of the annual chart, timing techniques, and astrological compatibility, but not the geometrically based lots.

CONCLUSION

This thesis has introduced the Mandaean astrological literature, as found in the *Sfar Malwašia*, into the discourse of the history of astrology and cross–cultural studies. The full story of the Mandaean origins may never be fully known, but they have left us valuable literature that expands our understanding of Gnosticism and the transmission of astrological techniques.

Pingree composes his narrative of the oriental–occidental transmission of astrology based on three types of evidence: self–reporting of sources by the authors, transliteration of technical terms, and what he calls "improbably complex theories" which are unlikely to have independent sources.[490] His model is appropriate for the analysis of the Mandaean astrological literature.

It has been demonstrated that the Mandaean use of mundane houses is a transitional point between the earliest Hellenistic topics and later Arabic topics. The institution of sepa-

---

[490] Pingree, *BTB*, 9.

rate horoscopes for men and women illustrates the beginnings of what is now called *astrological synastry*, or relationship compatibility. The mundane techniques may be the best examples of true Sassanian astrology surviving. In any case, the annual prognostications show the influence of many cultures that the Mandaeans had contact with. But the Mandaeans are non-conformist, and we have also seen variations in their astrological techniques that are truly unique to them alone.

Further research may show how the influence of Gnosticism and even the practices of the Essenes have modified and directed the use of astrology for individuals and communities across the Fertile Crescent. The Hebrew scholar John C. Reeves speculates that there is a connection between the Essenes, the Elkasaites, a Qumran sect called the "Ossaean," and another called "Sampsaeans" that might possibly be the origin of an eastern group that was given the name "Sabaean."[491] He writes:

> The popularity of Jewish pseudepigraphic traditions in the late antiquity and medieval Near East is not solely due to Manichaean efforts—there is ample attestation of similar preservative efforts and distinctive transformation with in Babylonian and Iranian Judaism, Harranian paganism, Mandaeism, Syrio–Mesopotamian Christianity, and Shi'I Islam. The ultimate results is a complex 'symbiosis' wherein Jewish, Christian, Zoroastrain, gnostic, and pagan currents feed off of and reinforce each other to form strange, hybrid ideological structures whose definitive statements are issued in highly mythologized tractates like *Sefer ha–Bahir* and *Ummn al–Kitab*.[492]

---

[491] Reeves, *Heralds of That Good Realm*, 47–8.

[492] Ibid., 48.

CONCLUSION

The great British explorer and orientalist Sir Richard Burton (1821–1890) commented, "History is silent upon that most interesting of subjects, the early connection of India and Egypt. There are, however, still traces of its existence through Arabia."[493] Neugebauer has written, "Following the unmistakable traces of very specific astrological doctrines, one can reconstruct the road which connected Hellenistic Mesopotamia with Hellenistic Egypt, with pre– Islamic Persia, and with India."[494] The Mandaean astrology found in the *Sfar Malwašia* helps to reconstruct that road.

---

[493] Sir Richard Francis Burton, *The Jew, The Gypsy and El Islam* (Chicago, IL: H. S. Stone & Company, 1898), 298.

[494] Neugebauer, The Exact Sciences in Antiquity, 172.

APPENDIX A

MAPS

The waterway formed after the Euphrates and Tigris rivers join is called *Shatt al-Arab*, or the River of the Arabs. The city of Basra is located on the Shatt al-Arab. The Mandaeans lived in the marshlands formed by the two rivers.

Map Credit: Public Domain, Central Intelligence Agency's World Factbook. 2005

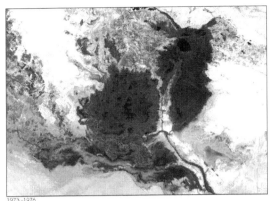

1973-1976

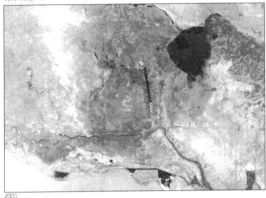

2000

Landsat satellite images of the Mesopotamian marshes. The top image is a composite image from 1973–1976 and the lower image was taken in 2000. The shrinking wetlands are indicated by black patches.

Map Credit: Public Domain, NASA.
http://earthobservatory.nasa.gov/IOTD/view.php?id=1716

APPENDIX B:

SAMPLE HOROSCOPES FROM THE *SFAR MALWAŠIA*

SAMPLE HOROSCOPE FOR A MAN

This will be the fate of one born in Scorpio…

(1ST HOUSE, ASCENDANT): If born at the beginning he belongs to Mars. He will be tall, slender, his eyes reddened, his hair straight and red, his face long and fair–skinned, and his neck long. His heart is hard and his disposition fiery, and from his works…. If born in the middle he will be under Sol. He will be of fair complexion and red haired. If at the end, he will be under Venus. He will be neither tall nor short, white–skinned, his eyebrows and hair black and thick, his limbs and his thighs are wide. He will endure hardship and be subject to terror, but will go to a healer and be cured. After a time, evil will cease to trouble him. He will be quick–tempered and swift to violence; his heart is fiery, and he will be contemptuous of deceitful persons. One hour he will rage with anger, and the next be calm. His brow will be strong and noble, and his lips full. He is quick of tongue and he aspires to that which he did not possess, and he seizes on the words that are in his heart. He will have eloquence and judgment; will be a wise man and pursue wisdom.

WITH A MONEY–BAG, SAGITTARIUS: He will not inherit family property, but his trade will be blessed. If not, for a number of years onwards he will use what is his and what is not. He will be made much of by a great man, a ruler, and will be employed in his service and find favor with him, and however old he is, he will work and grow rich. If the moon should be its third quarter, he will earn his bread everywhere and will acquire property from a far journey. Should the moon be absent or in its third quarter, he will be an amusing fellow and a jester. He will run like the wind and breathe like a dense cloud. They will malign him until he is thirty; subsequently he will grow rich and the older he gets the fairer his lot.

WITH BRETHREN, CAPRICORNUS: He will be stern, harsh, and domineering and will bring trouble on his brothers, on both those older and those younger than himself. One of his brothers will be involved in a quarrel. He will be reckless, and the cause of tribulations to his father and mother, and words from his mouth will injure his brothers, and his words are injurious. If Luna…in his parents' house is at its zenith, it will be well, and speedily, in a night.

WITH PARENTS, AQUARIUS: His father will survive but his mother perish. They shall give him mixed milk. For a space for 30 days he will bring ill–luck on his father and mother. His father will run off into the desert and will not remain in the dwelling of his fathers. Two fiery serpents will dwell in the place where he was born, and the sun will shine into it, and he will go in misery until he is 3 or 4 years old, bringing ill–fortune on his father and mother, and they will be ruined. If he is born at the end of his zodiacal sign, he will cause a breach between his father and mother.

WITH CHILDREN, PISCES: If the first–born of his children should be a son, he will be proud of him. If a daughter, it will be well for him…he will lose his children and will bring up strangers as his own (adopt). And one of the children will be scorched by fire, or sink in water and they will lift it out. If under Jupiter, he will rear sons and daughters, and slaves and handmaidens and his children will attain to great honor.

WITH PAINS AND BLEMISHES, ARIES: He will have an infirmity in a secret part of the body, and will have headache and earache. And in childhood he will be injured by boiling water, and fire will reach him, and he will be struck by an iron instrument, and he will have septic sores. He will have an affliction of the joints, and will experience an evil sickness, and a cauterizer will cauterize him, and he will be lamed by an iron weapon. In his youth he will have indigestion. He will eat and drink whilst planning evil in his heart.

WITH NUPTIALS, TAURUS: He will take three women to wife. The first woman will hold him ensnared for three days. If he takes a virgin, there will be strife at the wedding, or else one of his little ones will die. He asks for two women.

WITH DEATH, GEMINI: He lives many years and will have headache and (night) terrors, and will be wounded by iron and have pain in the eyes.

ABSENCE FROM HOME, CANCER: He will be blind of understanding and divulges to no one what is in his mind. He listens to talk as it actually was and repeats it as it was not, and perverts a part of it. He likes the society of others, but soon turns from them and approaches rulers.

IN CULMINATION, LEO: He will be brought into contact with noblemen and might kings, and will find favor with them. The older he gets, the more will he prosper.

WITH GOOD FORTUNE, VIRGO: So that he will be lucky, and will never stand suppliant at the gate of a friend, nor act meanly to a friend. He will go abroad unexpectedly, but his luck will protect him, his fame go out over land and water, and he will find favor.

WITH POOR FORTUNE, LIBRA: Sometimes he rejoices, and sometimes he is in trouble: good and evil are mingled together, and enemies pursue him with evil intent. Crucial years are: at 5 years old and illness—and from the time that he is 4 until he is seven he will be sickly; at 16, and illness; at 18, an illness; at 21, an illness, at 24, an illness; at 44, an illness; and at 62 an illness. If he gets over these illnesses he will live to be 68, and then go. *And Life is victorious...*

Sfar Malwašia 24-7.

SAMPLE HOROSCOPE FOR A WOMAN

This is what will become of the woman born in Libra...

(1ST HOUSE, ASCENDANT) She will not act falsely or evilly, nor will she oppress anyone, nor will she take anything that is not her own. Should she steal, for every one thing that she takes, seven will go from her. She will be an upright and honest woman and will live at peace. She will be tall of stature, her breast broad, and her hair thick. She will get a mark on her body. Her brows are long and fine and her eyes... (?). Her face is ruddy, her mouth small, and her father and mother are fond of her. Her temperament is warm, and people love her.

WITH A MONEY–BAG, SCORPIO: She will acquire much property but get nothing from her parents' estate. She will perform important work and will earn name and fame. She will be a dispenser of food and drink to others, and will ask no favors of her female friends. She will be comely. If under Luna, she will perform important work.

WITH BRETHREN, SAGITTARIUS: She will have brothers, and will remove herself from them. She will be struck by her brothers with an iron. She will be independent and hot—headed.

WITH PARENTS, CAPRICORNUS: It is her fate that for 63 days she will bring misfortune on herself, and for 20 days they must take her out to the country. If they do not treat her thus she will work harm.

WITH CHILDREN, AQUARIUS: So she will become pregnant and will bring forth. She will have beloved children. One daughter will have a mark on the mouth and will bring honor and joy and she will be fair.

WITH PAINS AND BLEMISHES, PISCES: She will have headache, and pain in the heart and belly, or will have swellings of the loins. She will be scalded by hot water.

WITH NUPTIALS, ARIES: She will be abducted from her home and become the property of a man of good family. If she goes through abduction, it will bring her misfortune and she will lose the first husband, and two or three men will be her lot. If Jupiter (the good!) star is in the ascendant, she will fall to the share of the first man.

WITH DEATH, TAURUS: She will live for many years, and when she dies, she will die of her heart and throat.

ABSENCE FROM HOME, GEMINI: So she will move from place to place and from house to house and will counter sorceries and turn them against those who made the. She will live agreeably.

IN CULMINATION, CANCER: It is her destiny to acquire possessions, and she will be fortunate, will own gold and silver, make a discovery and fair fortune will be hers.

WITH GOOD LUCK, LEO: It will come to pass that she will be blessed by fortune and that one hour she will be angry and the next appeased, and that she will be inflammable with men. She will have victuals and drink.

WITH POOR LUCK, VIRGO: She will have a fine house, but one woman will have access to her, and they will perform spells on her, and her reason will become darkened and her heart overthrown. Later on, she will have happiness. The dangerous years for her are: at 4 years old, an illness; at the ages of 8, 12, 18, 24, and 56, illnesses. If she gets over these illnesses, she will live to be 75 and then die.
And Life is victorious…

Sfar Malwaša 47-9.

BIBLIOGRAPHY

Abū Maʿshar. *Historical Astrology*. Translated by Keiji Yamamoto and Charles Burnett. Vol. 1, The Arabic Original. Islamic Philosophy, Theology, and Science. Leiden: Brill, 2000.

———. *The Abbreviation of the Introduction to Astrology (Arhat)*. Translated by Charles Burnett. Reston, VA: Arhat, 1997.

Agatharchides. *On the Erythraean Sea*. Translated by Stanley M. Burstein. London: The Hakluyt Society, 1989.

al–Bīrūnī. *The Book of Instruction in the Elements of the Art of Astrology*. Translated by R. Ramsay Wright. London: Luzac & Co., 1934.

———. *The Chronology of Ancient Nations*. Translated by C. Edward Sachau. London: William H. Allen and Co., 1879.

al–Hakim, Maslamah ibn Ahmad. *Picatrix: The Goal of the Wise*. Edited by William Kiesel. Translated by Hashem Atallah. Seattle: Ouroboros Press, 2002.

al–Kindi. *The Forty Chapters of Al–Kindi*. Translated by Benjamin Dykes. Minneapolis, MN: Cazimi Press, 2011.

al–Nadim. *The Fihrist, Two Volumes*. Translated by Bayard Dodge. 1st ed. New York: Columbia University Press, 1970.

Annus, M. "Some Otherworldly Journeys in Mesopotamian, Jewish, Mandaean and Yezidi Traditions." In *Of God(s), Trees, Kings, and Scholars: Neo–assyrian and Related Studies in Honour of Simo Parpola*, 315–26. Helsinki: Finnish Oriental Society, 2009.

Baigent, Michael. *From the Omens of Babylon*. First ed. London: Arkana, 1995.

Barton, Tamsyn. *Ancient Astrology*. London: Routledge, 1994.

Bell, Gertrude. *Arab War Lords and Iraqi Star Gazers: Gertrude Bell's The Arab of Mesopotamia*. Edited by Paul Rich. 2nd ed. Lincoln, NE: Authors Choice Press, 2001.

Ben–Dov, Jonathan. *Head of All Years: Astronomy and Calendars at Qumran in Their Ancient Context*. Leiden: Brill, 2008.

Bidmead, Julye. *The Akitu Festival: Religious Continuity and Royal Legitimation in Mesopotamia*. Piscataway, NJ: Gorgias Press, 2002.

Van Bladel, Kevin. *The Arabic Hermes: From Pagan Sage to Prophet of Science*. Oxford University Press, 2009.

Bonatti, Guido. *Liber Astronomiae, Books I, II, III with Index*. Translated by Robert Zoller and Rob Hand. Australia: Spica Publications, 1998.

Bottéro, Jean. *Mesopotamia: Writing, Reasoning, and the Gods*. Chicago, IL: University Of Chicago Press, 1995.

———. *Religion in Ancient Mesopotamia*. University Of Chicago Press, 2004.

Boyce, Mary. "On the Calendar of Zoroastrian Feasts." *Bulletin of the School of Oriental and African Studies* 33, no. 3 (1970): 513–539.

———. *Zoroastrians: Their Religious Beliefs and Practices*. London: Routledge & Kegan Paul Books, 1985.

Bradley, Richard. *The Significance of Monuments: On the Shaping of Human Experience in Neolithic and Bronze Age Europe*. New York: Routledge, 1998.

Brown, David. *Mesopotamian Planetary Astronomy–Astrology*. Groningen: Styx, 2000.

Buckley, Jorunn Jacobsen. "The Colophons in the Canonical Prayerbook of the Mandaeans." *Journal of Near Eastern Studies* 51, no. 1 (January 1992): 33–50.

———. *The Great Stem of Souls: Reconstructing Mandaean History.* Piscataway, NJ: Gorgias Press, 2005.

———. *The Mandaeans: Ancient Texts and Modern People.* Oxford University Press, 2002.

Bultmann, Rudolf. *Primitive Christianity in Its Contemporary Setting.* Translated by Reginald H. Fuller. (German Ed. 1949) 18th ed. Philadelphia: Fortress Press, 1980.

Burnett, Charles, Keiji Yamamoto, and Michio Yano. *Al-Qabīṣī (Alcabitius): The Introduction to Astrology.* London: The Warburg Institute, 2004.

Burton, Sir Richard Francis. *The Jew, The Gypsy and El Islam.* Chicago, IL: H. S. Stone & Company, 1898.

Campion, Nicholas. *Dawn of Astrology: A Cultural History of Western Astrology Volume One.* London: Continuum, 2008.

———. *The Great Year: Astrology, Millenarianism, and History in the Western Tradition.* First Printing. London: Penguin, 1995.

———. "The Possible Survival of Babylonian Astrology in the Fifth Century CE: A Discussion of Historical Sources." In *Horoscopes and Public Spheres,* edited by Günther Oestmann, H. Darrel Rutkin, and Kocku von Stuckrad, 69–92. Berlin: Walter de Gruyter, 2005.

Carnoy, Albert J. "Iranian Views of Origins in Connection with Similar Babylonian Beliefs." *Journal of the American Oriental Society* 36 (1916): 300–320.

Charak, Dr. K. S. *Essentials of Medical Astrology.* Delhi: Uma Publications, 1994.

Charlesworth, James H., ed. *The Old Testament Pseudepigrapha, Two Volumes.* Peabody, MA: Hendrickson, 2010.

Clay, Albert T. "The So–Called Fertile Crescent and Desert Bay." *Journal of the American Oriental Society* 44 (January 1, 1924): 186–201.

Cohen, Mark E. *The Cultic Calendars of the Ancient Near East.* Baltimore: CDL Publishers, 1993.

Collum, V.C.C. "Review: The Book of the Zodiac. by E. S. Drower." *Man* 51 (June 1, 1951): 85–86.

Corbin, Henry. *Spiritual Body and Celestial Earth.* Princeton, NJ: Princeton University Press, 1989.

Cumont, Franz. *Astrology and Religion Among the Greeks and Romans.* (1912) ed. New York: Dover, 1960.

Dalley, Stephanie. *Myths from Mesopotamia: Creation, the Flood, Gilgamesh, and Others.* Revised. Oxford University Press, 2009.

———. "The Influence of Mesopotamia Upon Israel and the Bible." In *The Legacy of Mesopotamia*, 57–83. Oxford: Oxford University Press, 1998.

———. "The Sassanian Period and Early Islam, C. AD 224–651." In *The Legacy of Mesopotamia*, 164–181. Oxford: Oxford University Press, 1998.

Dieleman, Jacco. "Stars and the Egyptian Priesthood." In *Prayer, Magic, and the Stars in the Ancient and Late Antique World*, edited by Scott Noegel, Joel Walker, and Brannon Wheeler, 137–53. University Park, PA: Pennsylvania State University Press, 2003.

Diodorus Siculus. *Library of History, Volume II, Books 2.35–4.58.* Translated by C. H. Oldfather. Loeb. Cambridge, MA: Harvard University Press, 1935.

Doniger, Wendy, and Brian K. Smith, trans. *The Laws of Manu*. Reprint. Penguin Books, 1991.

Dorotheus, and David Pingree. *Carmen Astrologicum*. Pingree's Preface trans. by Dorian Gieseler Greenbaum. Abingdon, MD: Astrology Classics Publishers, 2005.

Drower, E. S, and R Macuch. *A Mandaic Dictionary*. Oxford: Clarendon Press, 1963.

Drower, E. S. *The Secret Adam : A Study of Nasoraean Gnosis*. London: Oxford University Press, 1960.

Drower, E. S. *Diwan Abatur, or Progress Through the Purgatories*. Vatican City: Biblioteca Apostolica Vaticana, 1950.

———. *Lady E. S. Drower's Scholarly Correspondence: An Intrepid English Autodidact in Iraq*. Edited by Jorunn Jacobsen Buckley. Numen Book Series 137. Leiden: Brill, 2012.

———. "Mandaean Polemic." *Bulletin of the School of Oriental and African Studies, University of London* 25, no. 1/3 (January 1, 1962): 438–448.

———. *The Book of the Zodiac (Sfar Malwašia) D.C. 31*. Oriental Translation Fund XXXVI. London: The Royal Asiatic Society, 1949.

———. *The Haran Gawaita and the Baptism of Hibil–Ziwa*. Rome: Biblioteca Apostolica Vaticana, 1953.

———. "The Mandaean New Year Festival." *Man* 36 (November 1, 1936): 185–188.

———. *The Mandaeans of Iraq and Iran: Their Cults, Customs, Magic, Legends, and Folklore*. 1st ed. Oxford: Clarendon Press, 1937.

———. *Water into Wine*. John Murray Publishers Ltd, 1956.

Elukin, Jonathan. "Maimonides and the Rise and Fall of the Sabians: Explaining Mosaic Laws and the Limits of

Scholarship." *Journal of the History of Ideas* 63, no. 4 (October 2002): 619–637.

Fincke (Heidelberg), Jeanette C. "The Babylonian Texts of Nineveh." *Archiv Für Orientforschung*, no. 50 (2004 2003): 111–49.

Fleming, Daniel E. *Time at Emar: The Cultic Calendar & the Rituals from the Diviner's House (Mesopotamian Civilizations 11)*. Winona Lake, IN: Eisenbrauns, 2000.

Foster, Benjamin R. *From Distant Days: Myths, Tales, and Poetry of Ancient Mesopotamia*. Bethesda, MD: CDL Publishers, 1995.

Frothingham, A. L. *Stephen Bar Sudaili the Syrian Mystic, and the Book of Hierotheos*. Leyden [Leiden]: Brill, 1886.

Gordon, Cyrus H. *Before the Bible: The Common Background of Greek and Hebrew Civilisation*. London: Collins, 1962.

———. "Review: Handbook of Classical and Modern Mandaic by Rudolf Macuch." *Journal of Near Eastern Studies* 26, no. 2 (April 1, 1967): 133–135.

———. "Review: Mandaeism by Kurt Rudolph." *Journal of the American Oriental Society* 99, no. 3 (July 1, 1979): 476.

Green, H. S., Raphael, and Charles E. O. Carter. *Mundane Astrology: The Astrology of Nations and States*. New York: Astrology Center of America, 2005.

Green, T. M. *The City of the Moon God: Religious Traditions of Harran*. Leiden: Brill, 1997.

Greenbaum, Dorian Gieseler, and Micah T. Ross. "The Role of Egypt in the Development of the Horoscope." In *Egypt in Transition*, 146–181. Prague: Czech Institute of Egyptology, Faculty of Arts, Charles University in Prague, 2010.

Greenfield, J. C., and M. Sokoloff. "Astrological and Related Omen Texts in Jewish Palestinian Aramaic." *Journal of Near Eastern Studies* 48, no. 3 (July 1, 1989): 201–214.

Greenfield, Jonas C. "A Mandaic Miscellany." *Journal of the American Oriental Society* 104, no. 1 (January 1, 1984): 81–85.

———. "Review: A Pair of Nasoraean Commentaries. Translated by E. S. Drower." *Journal of the American Oriental Society* 90, no. 2 (April 1, 1970): 339–340.

Gündüz, Şinasi. *The Knowledge of Life: The Origins and Early History of the Mandaeans and Their Relations to the Sabians of the Qur'an and to the Harranians.* Oxford University Press, 1994.

Häberl, Charles G. "Review of Das Mandäische Fest Der Schalttage by Bogdan BurteaReview." *Journal of the American Oriental Society* 127, no. 2 (April 1, 2007): 208–210.

Hämeen–Anttila, Jaakko. *The Last Pagans of Iraq: Ibn Waḥshiyya And His Nabatean Agriculture.* Leiden: Brill, 2006.

Hand, Rob. *Whole Sign Houses The Oldest House System.* Reston, VA: Arhat, 2000.

Harvey, Charles, Nicholas Campion, and Michael Baigent. *Mundane Astrology: An Introduction to the Astrology of Nations & Groups.* Revised. London: Thorsons Publishers, 1992.

Hastings, James. *Encyclopaedia of Religion and Ethics.* Edinburgh: T. & T. Clark, 1908.

Henrichs, Albert. "Mani and the Babylonian Baptists: A Historical Confrontation." *Harvard Studies in Classical Philology* 77 (1973): 23–59.

————. "The Cologne Mani Codex Reconsidered." *Harvard Studies in Classical Philology* 83 (1979): 339–367.

Hesiod. *Works and Days.* Translated by Hugh G. Evelyn–White. Loeb. Cambridge, MA: Harvard University Press, 1914.

Holden, James Herschel. *A History of Horoscopic Astrology.* 2nd ed. Tempe, AZ: American Federation of Astrologers, Inc., 1996.

Hourani, George F., and John Carswell. *Arab Seafaring: In the Indian Ocean in Ancient and Early Medieval Times.* Expanded ed. Princeton University Press, 1995.

Hunger, Hermann, and David Pingree, trans. *MUL.APIN: An Astronomical Compendium in Cuneiform.* Archiv Für Orientforschung. Horn: Berger, 1989.

Ibn Ezra, Abraham. *The Beginning of Wisdom.* Edited by Rob Hand. Translated by Meira B. Epstein. Reston, VA: Arhat, 1998.

Jain, Manik Chand. *Mundane Astrology.* Delhi: Sagar Publications, 1992.

Jastrow, Morris. "Some Notes on 'The Monolith Inscription of Salmaneser II'." *Hebraica* 4, no. 4 (July 1, 1888): 244–246.

Jonas, Hans. *The Gnostic Religion: The Message of the Alien God and the Beginnings of Christianity.* 2nd ed. enlarged. Boston: Beacon Press, 1963.

Jones, Alexander. *Astronomical Papyri from Oxyrhynchus.* Philadelphia: American Philosophical Society, 1999.

Jowit, Juliette. "Paradise Found: Water and Life Return to Iraq's 'Garden of Eden'." *The Guardian.* UK, July 9, 2010. http://www.guardian.co.uk/world/2010/jul/09/iraq-marshes–reborn.

Juste, David. "Neither Observation nor Astronomical Tables: An Alternative Way of Computing the Planetary Longitudes in the Early Western Middle Ages." In *Studies in the History of the Exact Sciences in Honour of David Pingree*, 181–222. Leiden: Brill, 2004.

Keall, E. J. "Parthian Nippur and Vologases' Southern Strategy: A Hypothesis." *Journal of the American Oriental Society* 95, no. 4 (December 1975): 620–632.

Kennedy, E. S., and B. L. van der Waerden. "The World–Year of the Persians." *Journal of the American Oriental Society* 83, no. 3 (1963): 315–327.

Kennedy, E.S., and David Pingree. *The Astrological History of Māshā'allāh*. First ed. Cambridge, MA: Harvard University Press, 1971.

Kraeling, Carl H. *Anthropos and Son of Man: A Study in the Religious Syncretism of the Hellenistic Orient (1927)*. Eugene, OR: Wipf & Stock Publishers, 2008.

Legge, Francis. *Forerunners and Rivals of Christianity from 330 B.C. to 330 A.D., Two Volumes*. Hyde Park, NY: University Books, 1964.

Lehman, J. Lee. *Traditional Medical Astrology*. Atglen, PA: Schiffer Publishing, Ltd., 2011.

Lehoux, Daryn. *Astronomy, Weather, and Calendars in the Ancient World: Parapegmata and Related Texts in Classical and Near–Eastern Societies*. New York: Cambridge University Press, 2007.

Lilly, William. *Christian Astrology*. (London: 1647). Issaquah, WA: JustUs & Associates, 1997.

Link, Arthur E. "The Earliest Chinese Account of the Compilation of the Tripiṭaka (II)." *Journal of the American Oriental Society* 81, no. 3 (1961): 281–299.

Linssen, Marc J. H. *The Cults of Uruk and Babylon: The Temple Ritual Texts As Evidence for Hellenistic Cult Practises.* Leiden: Brill, 2003.

Lokamanya. *Vedic Chronology And Vedanga Jyotisha.* Translated by Bal Gangadhar Tilak. Poona City, India: Messrs Tilak Bros., 1925.

Luck, Georg. *Arcana Mundi.* Baltimore: Johns Hopkins University Press, 1986.

Lupieri, Edmondo. *The Mandaeans: The Last Gnostics.* Translated by Charles Hindley. American Edition (Italian ed. 1993). Italian Texts and Studies on Religion and Society. Cambridge, U.K.: William B. Eerdmans Publishing Company, 2002.

MacKenzie, D. N. "Zoroastrian Astrology in the 'Bundahišn'." *Bulletin of the School of Oriental and African Studies, University of London* 27, no. 3 (January 1, 1964): 511–529.

"Mandaean Human Rights Annual Report". Mandaean Human Rights Group, September 1022. http://www.mandaeanunion.org/HMRG/MHRG Annual Report 2011.pdf.

Manilius, M. *The Five Books of Manilius.* Translated by Thomas Creech. (London, 1697). American Federation of Astrologers, 1953.

"Māshā'allāh's Zoroastrian Historical Astrology." In *Horoscopes and Public Spheres,* 95–100. Berlin: Walter de Gruyter, 2005.

Maternus, Firmicus. *Matheseos Libri VIII.* Translated by Jean Rhys Bram. Reprint. Abingdon, MD: Astrology Classics, 1975.

McCullough, W.S. *Jewish and Mandaean Incantation Bowls in the Royal Ontario Museum*. Toronto, Canada: University of Toronto Press, 1967.

McEvilley, Thomas. *The Shape of Ancient Thought: Comparative Studies in Greek and Indian Philosophies*. 1st ed. Allworth Press, 2001.

McGrath, James F. "Misidentified Mandaic Manuscript." *Exploring Our Matrix*, September 28, 2009. http://www.patheos.com/blogs/exploringourmatrix/2009/09/misidentified–mandaic–manuscript.html.

Merlan, Philip. "Review: Gnosis Und Spätantiker Geist by Hans Jonas." *The Journal of Philosophy* 55, no. 17 (1958): 743–748.

Montgomery, James A. *Aramaic Incantation Texts from Nippur*. Philadelphia: University of Pennsylvania Museum, 1913.

Morony, Michael G. "Magic and Society in Late Sasanian Iraq." In *Prayer, Magic, and the Stars in the Ancient and Late Antique World*, edited by Scott Noegel, Joel Walker, and Brannon Wheeler, 83–107. University Park, PA: Pennsylvania State University Press, 2003.

Müller–Kessler, Christa. "The Mandaeans and the Question of Their Origin." *Aram* 16 (2004): 47–60.

Neelkantha. *Tajik*. Translated by D.P. Saxena. Delhi, India: Ranjan Publications, 2001.

Ness, Lester J. *Written In The Stars: Ancient Zodiac Mosaics*. Shangri La Publications Ltd, 1999.

Neugebauer, O., and H. B. Van Hoesen. *Greek Horoscopes*. Philadelphia: American Philosophical Society, 1987.

Neugebauer, O. *The Exact Sciences in Antiquity*. 2nd ed. New York: Dover, 1969.

Newmarker, Chris, and Associated Press. "Mandaeans Ponder Their Survival." *The Houston Chronicle*, February 10, 2007. http://www.chron.com/life/houston–belief/article/Mandaeans–ponder–their–survival–1629523.php.

Nickerson, Angela, Richard A Bryant, Robert Brooks, Zachary Steel, and Derrick Silove. "Fear of Cultural Extinction and Psychopathology Among Mandaean Refugees: An Exploratory Path Analysis." *CNS Neuroscience & Therapeutics* 15, no. 3 (2009): 227–236.

Nilsson, Martin P. *Primitive Time–reckoning; a Study in the Origins and First Development of the Art of Counting Time Among the Primitive and Early Culture Peoples.* Translated by F. J. Fielden. Lund: Biblolife, 1920.

North, J. D. *Horoscopes and History.* London: The Warburg Institute, 1986.

O'Flaherty, Wendy Doniger. *Hindu Myths: A Sourcebook Translated from the Sanskrit.* Penguin Classics, 1975.

Obermann, Julian. "Two Magic Bowls: New Incantation Texts from Mesopotamia." *The American Journal of Semitic Languages and Literatures* 57, no. 1 (January 1, 1940): 1–31.

Pallis, Svend Aage. *Mandaean Studies.* 2nd ed. Amsterdam: Philo Press, 1926.

Parpola, Simo. *Letters from Assyrian and Babylonian Scholars.* Vol. X. Helsinki University Press, 1993.

Paulus, Alexandrinus. *Late Classical Astrology: Paulus Alexandrinus and Olympiodorus.* Edited by Rob Hand. Translated by Dorian Gieseler Greenbaum. Reston, VA: Arhat, 2001.

Petermann, Julius. *The Great Treasure or Great Book, Commonly Called "The Book of Adam," The Ginzā.* Edited by Charles Häberl. Piscataway, NJ: Gorgias Press, 2007.

Pingree, David. "Antiochus and Rhetorius." *Classical Philology* 72, no. 3 (July 1, 1977): 203–223.

———. "Astronomy and Astrology in India and Iran." *Isis* 54, no. 2 (June 1, 1963): 229–246.

———. *From Astral Omens to Astrology: From Babylon to Bīkāner*. Rome: Italiano per l'Africa e l'Oriente, 1997.

———. "The Indian Iconography of the Decans and Horâs." *Journal of the Warburg and Courtauld Institutes* 26, no. 4 (1963): 223–254.

———. *The Thousands of Abū Ma'shar*. London: The Warburg Institute, 1968.

———. *The Yavanajataka of Sphujidhvaja*. Cambridge, MA: Harvard University Press, 1978.

———. *Vrddhayavanajataka of Minaraja: Vol. II*. Baroda: Oriental Institute, 1976.

Popović, Mladen. *Reading the Human Body*. Leiden: Brill, 2007.

Pourshariati, Parvaneh. *Decline and Fall of the Sasanian Empire: The Sasanian–Parthian Confederacy and the Arab Conquest of Iran*. London: I. B. Tauris, 2008.

Powell, Robert. *History of the Zodiac*. Sophia Academic Press, 2006.

Ptolemy. *Tetrabiblos*. Translated by F. E. Robbins. Loeb. Cambridge, MA: Harvard University Press, 1940.

Ramesey, William. *Astrologie Restored (in Four Books)*. London: Printed for Robert White, 1653.

Rawlinson, George. *The Seven Great Monarchies of the Ancient Eastern World: The Seventh Monarchy: History of the Sasanian or New Persian Empire*, 1884.

Rawlinson, Henry C. "Royal Asiatic Society. Proceedings of the Fifty–First Anniversary Meeting of the Society, Held on the 18th of May, 1874." *Journal of the Royal Asiatic Society of Great Britain and Ireland* 7, no. 1. New Series (January 1, 1875): I–XXVII.

Reeves, John C. *Heralds of That Good Realm: Syro–Mesopotamian Gnosis and Jewish Traditions.* Leiden: Brill, 1996.

Reiner, Erica. *Astral Magic in Babylonia.* Philadelphia: American Philosophical Society, 1995.

Robson, Eleanor. "Scholarly Conceptions and Quantifications of Time in Assyria and Babylonia, C.570–250 BCE." In *Time and Temporality in the Ancient World*, 45–90. Philadelphia: University of Pennsylvania Museum of Archaeology and Anthropology, 2004.

Rochberg, Francesca. *In the Path of the Moon: Babylonian Celestial Divination and Its Legacy.* Leiden: Brill, 2010.

———. *The Heavenly Writing: Divination, Horoscopy, and Astronomy in Mesopotamian Culture.* New York: Cambridge University Press, 2004.

Rochberg–Halton, F. "Between Observation and Theory in Babylonian Astronomical Texts." *Journal of Near Eastern Studies* 50, no. 2 (April 1, 1991): 107–120.

———. "Elements of the Babylonian Contribution to Hellenistic Astrology." *Journal of the American Oriental Society* 108, no. 1 (January 1, 1988): 51–62.

———. "New Evidence for the History of Astrology." *Journal of Near Eastern Studies* 43, no. 2 (April 1, 1984): 115–140.

Rudolph, Kurt. *Gnosis: The Nature and History of Gnosticism.* Translated by P. W. Coxon, K. H. Kuhn, R. Wilson. Vol. (German 2nd ed. 1980). Edinburgh: T. & T. Clark, 1984.

Saheeh International, trans. *The Quran.* English. Saheeh International, 1997.

Schmidt, Francis. "Ancient Jewish Astrology: An Attempt to Interpret 4QCryptic (4Q186)." translated by Jeffrey M. Green. Jerusalem (École Pratique des Hautes Études, Paris): The Orion Center for the Study of the Dead Sea Scrolls and Associated Literature, 1996. http://orion.mscc.huji.ac.il/symposiums/1st/papers/Schmidt96.html#fn1.

Scott, James M. *On Earth as in Heaven: The Restoration of Sacred Time and Sacred Space in the Book of Jubilees.* Leiden: Brill, 2005.

Scurlock, JoAnn. "Sorcery in the Stars: STT 300, BRM 4.19–20 and the Mandaic Book of the Zodiac." *Archiv Für Orientforschung* 51 (2006 2005): 125–146.

Segal, J. B. "Obituary: Ethel Stefana, Lady Drower (1 December 1879–27 January 1972)." *Bulletin of the School of Oriental and African Studies,* 35, no. 3 (1972): 621–622.

———. "Review: The Haran Gawaita and the Baptism of Hibil–Ziwa by E. S. Drower." *Bulletin of the School of Oriental and African Studies, University of London* 18, no. 2 (January 1, 1956): 373–375.

Sela, Shlomo. *Abraham Ibn Ezra Book of the World.* Vol. Two. Leiden: Brill, 2009.

Selin, Helaine, ed. *Encyclopaedia of the History of Science, Technology, and Medicine in Non–Westen Cultures.* 1st ed. Boston, MA: Kluwer Academic, 1997.

Sokoloff, M. *A Dictionary of Jewish Babylonian Aramaic.* Baltimore: Johns Hopkins University Press, 2002.

Stewart, Rory. *The Prince of the Marshes: And Other Occupational Hazards of a Year in Iraq.* Orlando. FL: Harcourt, 2006.

Stol, Marten. "Review: Local Power in Old Babylonian Mesopotamia by Andrea Seri." *Journal of the American Oriental Society* 127, no. 2 (April 1, 2007): 212–215.

Stoyanov, Yuri. *The Other God: Dualist Religions from Antiquity to the Cathar Heresy.* London: Yale University Press, 2000.

Talmon, Shemaryahu, Jonathan Ben–Dov, and Uwe Glessmer. *Qumran Cave 4: XVI: Calendrical Texts.* Oxford: Oxford University Press, 2002.

Taqizadeh, S. H. "An Ancient Persian Practice Preserved by a Non–Iranian People." *Bulletin of the School of Oriental Studies, University of London* 9, no. 3 (January 1, 1938): 603–619.

Thapar, Romila. *Early India: From the Origins to AD 1300.* Berkeley, CA: University of California Press, 2004.

Thesiger, Wilfred. *Marsh Arabs.* London: Penguin Books, 1967.

Thorndike, Lynn. *A History of Magic and Experimental Science, Vol. 1.* New York: Columbia University Press, 1929.

Varāhamihira. *Brihat Jataka.* Translated by Prof. P.S. Sastri. Delhi: Ranjan Publications, 1995.

Varisco, Daniel Martin. *Medieval Agriculture and Islamic Science: The Almanac of a Yemeni Sultan.* Seattle: University of Washington Press, 1994.

Vitruvius. *The Ten Books on Architecture.* Translated by Morris Hicky Morgan. Cambridge, MA: Harvard University Press, 1914. http://www.gutenberg.org/files/20239/20239–h/29239–h.htm.

Widengren, Geo. *Mesopotamian Elements in Manichaeism.* Studies in Manichaean, Mandaean, and Syrian–gnostic Religion (King and Saviour Seris No. 2). Uppsala: Lundequistska bokhandeln, 1946.

Yamamoto, K., and Charles Burnett. *Abū Maʿshar on Historical Astrology: The Book of Religions and Dynasties on Great Conjunctions, Two Volumes.* Leiden: Brill, 2000.

Yamauchi, Edwin M. "Aramaic Magic Bowls." *Journal of the American Oriental Society* 85, no. 4 (October 1, 1965): 511–523.

———. *Mandaic Incantation Texts.* Piscataway, NJ: Gorgias Press, 2005.

———. *Pre–Christian Gnosticism: A Survey of the Proposed Evidences.* Grand Rapids, MI: William B. Eerdmans Publishing Company, 1973.

———. "The Present Status of Mandaean Studies." *Journal of Near Eastern Studies* 25, no. 2 (April 1, 1966): 88–96.

Zaehner, R. C. *Zurvan: A Zoroastrian Dilemma.* Reprint. New York: Bibio and Tannen, 1955.

Zarins, Juris. "The Early Settlement of Southern Mesopotamia: A Review of Recent Historical, Geological, and Archaeological Research." *Journal of the American Oriental Society* 112, no. 1 (January 1, 1992): 55–77.

Zerubavel, Eviatar. *The Seven Day Circle.* New York: Free Press, 1985.

Zoller, Robert. "Abū Maʿshar: Prince of Astrologers", revised 2000 1993. http://www.new-library.com/zoller/features/rz–article–abumashar.shtml.

———. *The Arabic Parts in Astrology: A Lost Key to Prediction.* New York: Inner Traditions, 1989.

ABOUT THIS BOOK

This is an abridged edition of the MA thesis written in 2012 by Maire M. Masco. The thesis discusses the genethlialogical and mundane astrological techniques found in the *Sfar Malwasia*, or Mandaean "Book of the Zodiac."

ABOUT THE AUTHOR

Masco writes on the history of astrology. Her articles have been published in the U.S., Australia, and India. She lectures internationally on East/West religious traditions, Jyotisha astrology, and observational astronomy. Masco lives in Tacoma, WA.

40119223R00095

Made in the USA
Lexington, KY
25 March 2015